The Bully in the Book and in the Classroom

C. J. Bott

D1127940

The Scarecrow Press, Inc.
Lanham, Maryland • Toronto • Oxford
2004

SCARECROW PRESS, INC.

Published in the United States of America
by Scarecrow Press, Inc.
A wholly owned subsidiary of
The Rowman & Littlefield Publishing Group, Inc.
4501 Forbes Boulevard, Suite 200, Lanham, Maryland 20706
www.scarecrowpress.com

PO Box 317
Oxford
OX2 9RU, UK

British Library Cataloguing in Publication Information Available

Library of Congress Cataloging-in-Publication Data

Bott, C. J. (Christie Jo), 1947–
The bully in the book and in the classroom / C. J. Bott.
p. cm.
Includes bibliographical references and index.
ISBN 0-8108-5048-6 (pbk. : alk. paper)
1. Bullying in schools—Prevention. 2. Bullying in schools—Bibliography.
3. Bullying in schools—Abstracts. I. Title.
LB3013.3.B68 2005
371.5'8—dc22

2004008536

™ The paper used in this publication meets the minimum requirements of American National Standard for Information Sciences—Permanence of Paper for Printed Library Materials, ANSI/NISO Z39.48-1992.
Manufactured in the United States of America.

To my three sisters, Nancy, Betsy, and Becky, for filling my childhood with happy, silly, and empowering moments that gave me the strength to face the outside world.

And to our parents who loved all of us, all the time—no small task.

Contents

List of Illustrations

Cover Image from *Hands Are Not for Hitting* by Martine Agassi, Ph. D. © 2000. Used with permission from Free Spirit Publishing Inc., Minneapolis, MN. 1-866-703-7322; www.freespirit.com. All rights reserved. p. 18.

STAND TALL, MOLLY LOU MELON © 2001 by Patty Lowell, Illustrations © 2001 by David Catrow. Used with permission of Scholastic Press. p.19.

NOBODY KNEW WHAT TO DO: A STORY ABOUT BULLYING by Becky Ray McCain. Illustration © 2001 by Todd Leonardo. Used with the permission of Albert Whitman & Company. p. 20.

WINGS © 2000 by Christopher Myers. Used with permission of Scholastic Press. p. 21.

THE RECESS QUEEN © 2002 by Alexis O'Neill, Illustrations © 2002 by Laura Huliska-Beith. Used with permission of Scholastic Press. p. 23.

Mr. Lincoln's Way, copyright 2001 Patricia Polacco. Reprinted by permission of Philomel Books, a division of Penguin Young Readers Group, a member of Penguin Group (USA) Inc. p. 24.

JAKE DRAKE BULLY BUSTER © 2001 by Andrew Clements. Illustrations © 2001 Amanda Harvey. Aladdin Paperbacks, an imprint of Simon & Schuster Children's Publishing. Used with permission. p. 29.

MIGUEL LOST & FOUND IN THE PALACE © 2002 by Barbara Beasley Murphy. Illustration for cover art by George Ancona. Used with permission of Museum of New Mexico Press. p. 59.

Agnes Parker . . . Girl In Progress, copyright 2003 Charise Mericle Harper. Reprinted by permission of Dial Books for Young Readers, a division of Penguin Young Readers Group, a member of Penguin Group (USA) Inc. p. 62.

Jacket of ADDY LEARNS A LESSON: A SCHOOL STORY by Connie Porter, illustrations by Melodye Rosales. © 1993 by Pleasant Company, Inc. Printed by Scholastic. Used with permission of Scholastic Press. p. 64.

Cover Image from *Bullies Are a Pain in the Brain* by Trevor Romain © 1997. Used with permission from Free Spirit Publishing Inc., Minneapolis, MN. 1-866-703-7322; www.freespirit.com. All rights reserved. p. 67.

MANIAC MAGEE © 1990 by Jerry Spinelli. Cover © 1992 by HarperCollins Publishers. Used with permission of HarperCollins Publishers, Inc. p. 70.

Excerpts from TANGERINE © 1997 Edward Bloor, reprinted by permission of Harcourt, Inc. p. 80.

THE SKIN I'M IN © 1998 Sharon G. Flake, Jacket illustration © 1998 by Mark Havriliak. Used with permission of Disney/Hyperion Books for Children. p. 83.

THE MISFITS © 2001 by James Howe. Jacket illustrations © 2001 by Bagram Ibatoulline. Atheneum Books for Young Readers, an imprint of Simon & Schuster Children's Publishing. Used with permission from Bagram Ibatoulline. p. 86.

The Girls, copyright 2000 Amy Goldman Koss. Reprinted by permission of Dial Books for Young Readers, a division of Penguin Young Readers Group, a member of Penguin Group (USA) Inc. p. 89.

THE LOSERS' CLUB by John Lekich. © 2002 John Lekich. Used with permission of Annick Press. p. 92.

Preface

If a student is afraid of being picked on, bullied, or harassed because that student is from a different culture; is female; has a different shade of skin; speaks with a stutter or a foreign or regional accent; is older or younger; practices an unfamiliar religion or a minority sexual orientation; is too tall, short, thin, heavy, wears glasses; has too many pimples; doesn't understand as quickly as the other students; has an intense relationship with a computer; wears secondhand clothes, all black clothes, or cheap tennis shoes; or has hair that stands straight up and is midnight blue, that student will not be able to fully operate in the school environment. So without trying any of your skills, you face failure—because like that student, you cannot do your job in an atmosphere of fear.

Acknowledgments

My appreciation and thanks to:

Editors: Ed Kurdyla, Melissa Ray, and Karen Gray, the most patient in the land, at Scarecrow Press; Linda Benson and Cathi Dunn McCrae at VOYA;

Publishers: who graciously gave me permissions and books about bullies;

Friends, who have waited patiently for me to be available again, and Connie Caporuscio, who supported me through it all;

Our Young Adult Reading Group who brought me titles and listened to me talk about bully books no matter what our assigned topic;

Willing teachers and students particularly at Carylwood School in Bedford City Schools, Ohio, and Solon Middle School in Solon City Schools, Ohio;

Students, like Dennis Cummings and Terryle Davis, whose determination to be writers inspired me;

The entire staff at Global Issues Resource Center at Cuyahoga Community College;

Librarians like Linda Sleeman who pulls titles out of her magic hat, Linda Boydreff, my Internet resource, and Patty Campbell for her sage advice;

Abby L. Hoffmann and Phil Smith, my computer wizards;

Rick Ware and Helen Byrdsong, two amazing human spirits that influence my professional and personal life daily;

Don Gallo, my first reader, live-in editor, best friend and husband;

And everyone who told me a personal bully story and validated the need for this book.

Introduction

I was bullied as a child—nothing serious, but I kept it a secret and felt it was my fault. Because I had polio in the first grade, I missed the first semester and could never go out for recess that year. I became unsure of how to fit in. I was an easy target. Later, when I was asked to babysit my three younger sisters whenever my parents went out, I was a bully, not something I am proud of. But the times I remember clearest are the ones when I saw bullying and did nothing or contributed to the event through my silence.

Whenever I have wanted to get a point across subtly to my students, I have looked to books dealing with that specific social behavior. Children's literature and young adult literature have never let me down. The difference between teaching about bullying using this literature or the classics compares to teaching my classes speaking in English or speaking in Greek—I had no Greek students. One young adult book creates a more complete connection. Adults wrote the classics about other adults and to be read by adults, usually the well-educated and somewhat elite. Not so with books written for children and teens. These books translate right off the page and into the daily lives of most students.

I have been addicted to books written for young adults since I read *The Outsiders* by S. E. Hinton (a major bully book, by the way). These books present life lessons with humor, sensitivity, and timeliness. Even reluctant readers will read about the young person who is experiencing the same traumas as they are.

About eight years ago, I read *Hostile Hallways*, a research report done by the American Association of University Women. Though that report focused on sexual harassment, it prompted me to start my own research into bullying.

Bullying is the collective term that covers all forms of harassment and often without the bells and whistles that sexual harassment or racism stirs up. At that point the research I was reading proved that there was a need to address this issue—but they offered no solutions. Then I moved on to teacher curricula. There are hundreds of help books out there for teachers, counselors, administrators, and parents.

While all of this was percolating in my head, I was still reading YA literature, and the crossover was apparent. As a reader, I have always found myself in the pages of books; my students could too, if given the right books. My list of bully books started to grow. Bullies, targets, and bystanders live in picture books, chapter books, and teenage books, just as they live in every school around the world. Maybe our students should meet the bully in the book, and then they will recognize the bully in the classroom, along with the targets and the bystanders.

I offer titles of books dealing with bullying for people in grades K–12. Each chapter has a short introduction, 8–10 spotlights books with in-depth summaries, topics for discussion, and quotes for readers' response, and finally a bibliography of selected titles published from 1990 until this book went to print. I have read every book listed here and wish there was time to have read more. I leave the research for the researchers. They have proven the problem exists. I just happen to believe that literature written specifically for these ages is one of the best anti-bullying programs around.

Chapter One

The Bully, the Target, the Witness

"Bullying" is the new buzzword in our lives. In the USA it is neither possible nor wise to ignore this social enigma. Newspapers and magazines carry articles about what is happening, has happened, and needs to happen. Every talk show has interviewed experts and therapists to explain the problem, increase awareness, and offer guidelines. Bookstores and libraries have titles falling off the shelves. A person must actively hide to avoid awareness of this growing problem.

Bullying exists around the world. The Canadian based Internet site, www.bullying.org, provides articles about bullying in many countries, from Australia to Scotland. Research in this area began as early as the 1970s in Scandinavia. In 1983, Norway's Minister of Education launched a nationwide campaign dealing with bullying problems in schools, which followed shortly after three young boys (10 to 13 years old) committed suicide in what appeared to be the result of severe bullying by peers. Dan Olweus,[1] Professor of Psychology at the University of Bergen, Norway, has become recognized as the world's leading authority on bullying and victimization. This problem does not just exist in American schools.

Part of the reason for this heightened level of awareness is that we all have bully stories of our own. Each of us has either been the victim of cruel words, stories, actions, or has witnessed, usually with personal relief, someone else's torture. We remember and can still feel some of those emotions; they pop into our consciousness and constrict our stomachs with flashbacks triggered by a word, a look on someone's seemingly silent face, or a scenario from our favorite television show.

Ironically, the bullies are the last to remember those long ago events. Some will never see or accept their role in the harassment—because they are still doing what has always worked for them. They have just moved on to subtler, more sophisticated, and more defended strategies. Each of the three roles—the bully, the target or victim, and the witness or bystander—needs to be looked at closely. The target and the witnesses need empowering skills, and the bully needs awakening and alternative behaviors to fulfill his (her) needs.

Boys and girls both bully. We are familiar with the direct bullying ways boys use, usually physical and "in your face, right here, right now!" attitude. There is a sense of immediacy. Girls tend to choose a different and nearly undetectable form of bullying. Though these girls appear to be nice, they subtly humiliate the target with whispers in hallways, anonymous notes on lockers or desktops, exclusion from group gatherings, or demeaning errands assigned in pretext of allowing the target to pass the initiation needed to join the group. These behaviors are much harder for school staff to witness and confront. The harassers are often some of the leaders of the school and the teachers' helpers.

In *Odd Girl Out, The Hidden Culture of Aggression in Girls*, Rachel Simmons talks about these acts of alternative aggressions and breaks them down to relational, indirect, and social aggression.[2] In relational aggression, the bully uses the relationship to barter for power or control. The target is held captive and must face the if-you-were-my-friend-you-would-do-this attitude. With indirect aggression, the bully works behind the scene to harass the target, but publicly shows support. Excluding someone "accidentally" from an event and spreading rumors are two examples of this form of girl aggression. Social aggression is behavior that hurts the target's self-confidence and/or social position. There is overlap in these behaviors. The thing to remember is girls bully differently than boys: Females are sneaky about it, and their behavior can go on for a long time.

In the young adult (YA) novel, *The Girls* by Amy Goldman Koss,[3] Candace rules a group of five middle-school girls. Maya, new to the school, is thrilled to be included. Candace has picked her and that gives Maya immediate status, but when the other four have a sleep-over without her, Maya realizes she has fallen out of Candace's favor. Frantically, she tries to remember what she has said or done to offend Candace; maybe it was the sweater she wore, since Candace had commented negatively on it. During the sleepover, the other girls' discomfort over Maya's exclusion is hidden as they all follow Candace's lead.

Through the book, Koss lets readers see the girls' insecurities, in themselves and with their delicate status in the group.

Another book that portrays the rigidity of girl cliques comes from Australia. In *Walking Naked* by Alyssa Brugman,[4] the target is outside of the group. Megan and her friends, the top group of junior girls who are focused on grades and sports, torment Perdita in the hallways. They ignore her and refuse to make eye contact with her. However, as she passes, her head down and books clutched to her chest, the girls chant "Freak, Freak, Freak" just loudly enough for her to hear but not the teachers.

As a teacher of many years, I realize I had subconsciously created a profile for targets. The individual in the class whose voice I rarely hear, who sits on the edge of the room, in the back, on the side, or alone, is often smaller but could be larger. They wear less fashionable clothes, and their hair is less fashionably styled. Targets in both genders tend to be quieter than most students and try to avoid drawing attention. They have learned to walk down the halls without making eye contact with anyone. They strive to be invisible. My readings have taught me these are the passive victims. This is the image which comes to most of our minds when we hear the word "victim."

When I have talked with my students about bullying, someone always asks, "What about the kid who deserves to be picked on?" This student is easy to trick into reacting; other students often set him up to get in trouble or look foolish. Because these students do not know how to interact with other teens, they play a part in the problem. A student diagnosed with Attention Deficit Hyperactive Disorder (ADHD) may have an energy level that wears down other students as quickly as it wears down the teacher. Sometimes students with Tourette's syndrome fit here. All of these are the provocative victims. They cannot help themselves, but they do not deserve to be picked on. The perfect example of a provocative victim is Joey Pigza in the award-winning *Joey Pigza* trilogy by Jack Gantos.[5] Joey introduces himself with "At school they say I'm wired bad, or wired mad, or wired sad, or wired glad, depending on my mood and what teacher has ended up with me."[6] He wants to be good but he just cannot help himself. In all my teacher preparation, nothing helped me understand an ADHD student more than reading this book. It is fiction, but it has changed the way I work in reality.

The majority of our students are not bullies or targets, but they are witnesses. They see the harassment and respond to it in a variety of ways; each of these behaviors connects the witness to the harassing act.

Barbara Coloroso uses Dan Olweus's Bullying Circle in her book *The Bully, The Bullied and the Bystander*. She discusses the bystanders' roles as Followers, Supporters, Passive Supporters, Disengaged Onlookers, Possible Defenders, and the ever-rare Defender of the Target.[7]

Many of these roles can be seen in *Rat*, by Jan Cheripko.[8] Coach Stennard, the basketball coach, was caught sexually assaulting Cassandra Diaz, the captain of the cheerleaders. Jeremy Chandler walks in on the event, and his presence allows Cassandra to escape. Jeremy, the team manager, knows it is wrong and even though the coach threatens him, he tells—first his parents and then the administration. He has to testify in court. The basketball team had been last year's district champions and had expected to repeat that this season. Now as their coach is convicted, they blame Jeremy and Cassandra instead of Coach Stennard. Simpson Theodore, always angry and aggressive, steps into the role of main tormentor. A few of the team members become bully supporters with comments that encourage Simpson in his verbal and physical torment of Jeremy. A few other players are passive supporters. They watch Simpson hit Jeremy with a basketball in mid jump and see Jeremy crumple to the floor, but they do nothing. When an adult asks what is going on, they look away. Most of the school body behaves as disengaged onlookers. Their attitude seems to imply, "That's a basketball problem, it doesn't concern us." Even the school board says, "Let's put this behind us and forget it." They do not recognize and honor Jeremy's courage. On the team, there are a few players who are possible defenders. Two are friends of Cassandra and members of "parallel cultures,"[9] and that may have something to do with their heightened sensitivity. Their voices and actions become stronger as the story continues and they earn their way into defender of the target status. On some level, every guy on the team knew Coach Stennard was wrong, that what he did was a violation of trust on many levels. But they would rather torment Jeremy than publicly accept that truth. For the rest of their fictional lives, they will have to live with their behavior.

The longer I teach and the more I research bullying, the more I am amazed by what people will do to protect their own status, whether as a group leader or a member or the victim desperate for invisibility. They will give up their morals, integrity, money, friends, family members, or self-respect in their fear of the bully. That act empowers the bully like none other.

The reasons these witnesses do not intervene are not surprising to anyone who has worked with kids: they are afraid. They could get hurt, they could become the bully's next target, or they could make everything worse. Also, these witnesses, like too many adults, do not know what to do.

Adults, however, have certain responsibilities, and looking the other way should not be one of them. Those of us who work in schools must do our best to create a safe zone, whether that zone is a classroom, an office, a library, a bus, a locker room, or a playground. Just like the students, we cannot do our best in an atmosphere of fear.

There are many more witnesses of bullying and harassment than there are bullies and targets. Teaching books like *The Girls, Walking Naked, Joey Pigza Swallowed the Key,* or *Rat* and letting our students talk out the incidents at a safe, objective level lets them form and practice their beliefs and morals before they are called into action. After such a dialogue, ignoring the bully will never be as easy. Students and adults need to be aware of the responsibility that comes with their choice of action or silence.

Notes

1. Dan Olweus, *Bullying At School: What We Know and What We Can Do.* (Oxford, UK.: Blackwell Publishers, 1993), 2.

2. Rachel Simmons, *Odd Girl Out: The Hidden Culture of Aggression in Girls.* (New York: Harcourt, 2002).

3. Amy Goldman Koss, *The Girls.* (New York: Dial, 2000).

4. Alyssa Brugman, *Walking Naked.* (New York: Delacorte Press, 2004).

5. Jack Gantos, *Joey Pigza Swallowed the Key.* (New York: Farrar, Straus & Giroux, 1998).

———. *Joey Pigza Loses Control.* (New York: Farrar, Straus & Giroux, 2000).

———. *What Would Joey Do?* (New York: Farrar, Straus & Giroux, 2002).

6. *Joey Pigza Swallowed the Key,* 3.

7. Barbara Coloroso, *The Bully, the Bullied and the Bystander.* (New York: HarperCollins, 2003), 64-67.

8. Jan Cheripko, *Rat.* (Honesdale, PA: Boyds Mills Press, 2002).

9. I attended a Virginia Hamilton Conference and heard those words, "parallel cultures." Hamilton chose to use that term over "minority cultures."

Chapter Two

What Teachers Can Do— Need to Do

Teachers usually do nothing about bullying. Research shows it, kids say it, and many teachers will admit it. I admit it. The first ten years of my teaching career I did little about bullying unless it was blatant and in my classroom. The hallways were a different world—no one was in charge there. But somewhere during these last twenty years, I started feeling protective of my students. I wanted my classroom to be a safe space, a place where the kids would feel comfortable and free from harassment. Actually, like you, I want that to exist in the entire school environment, but making that happen for the whole building seemed too big to attempt—there were too many obstacles. However, it was possible to break down that huge task and confront some of the smaller problems that I could influence.

The ideal bully prevention program should exist on three levels: the classroom, the building, and the district. Each level has its own boundaries and characteristics, though some ingredients are the same. The smaller environment involves fewer people, which makes it easier to impact people's behavior. The larger environment has more complicated components, as there are more variables. But one of the jobs at all three levels in a school system is to keep students safe from harm. The easiest place to start is in the individual classroom with usually one willing teacher and a group of students.

The Individual Classroom

As individual teachers, we are in charge of our own classroom; it is our space to live in with our students for the year. We can begin building respectful environments by setting class rules for behavior and posting them on the bulletin board. Usually students can and should help create these guidelines, and their ownership through this involvement will go a long way toward establishing and helping to monitor appropriate behavior. Even the youngest children will tell us how we should treat each other. (Most of their parents have worked long and hard on "Let's share.")

Once the class guidelines are clearly stated and displayed in my class, my responsibility is to support them. (My district later made an "Acceptance Poster" from my guidelines and distributed it throughout the high school, the middle school, and the intermediate school.) The more completely I weave these expectations into our everyday activities, the more my students equate them with our classroom and with me. As they become part of my reputation, my behavior changes to reinforce these expectations. The word gets out—before, during, after school, in my classes, in the hallways—"Nobody picks on anybody if Ms. Bott is there." I am sure some harassment happened on my watch, but I hope some problems are avoided because of this early work. I hope that when they leave my classroom, each student carries these same concepts to the outside world.

Name-calling is the most common form of bullying, and one we witness from kindergarten to senior year. That old saying, "Sticks and stones may break my bones, but words will never hurt me" is a lie. James Howe, a wise and realistic voice in young people's literature, says in *The Misfits*,[1] "Sticks and stones may break our bones, but words will break our spirit." Because I taught in a high school, the names I heard in the hallways were stronger than those heard in elementary buildings. My students and I talked about all the words that cut people down. *Nigger, bitch, and faggot* were the most incendiary and the first ones mentioned. The students who approved of using these words heard from the students who did not, and there were many of them—suddenly an awakening! True to their age, each believed she or he talked for everyone the same age. Eventually we set some ground rules, using the word "respect" a lot.

"Respect" and "disrespect" are two words that carry an enormous amount of power with students. I do not know when the word "disrespect" (or just "dis") crossed over from a noun to a verb, but to direct that word at someone is like challenging him to a duel. The basic need to be respected, recognized, and honored for the "humanness" in each of us crosses all boundaries of race, religion, gender, sexual orientation, economic level, educational level, and intellectual ability. Respect touches each of us and unites all of us.

My sophomores became so aware of their language that after someone would slip, another student would simply point to the Acceptance Poster and apologies would follow. After a similar discussion with my seniors, each wrote a paper on "The Power of Words." Choosing a word that had carried intensity throughout their lives, and in many cases still had the capacity to cause pain, they wrote about how that word had affected them. The words ranged from *stupid, dummy, skinny, fat, or retard* in the earlier grades to real hate slurs in the older grades. Several students privately told me about being called these words day after day by other kids at school and of the emotional scars and bruises that they still carried from being shamed by those names.

Classroom environments are powerful places, and sometimes the teacher's view of the classroom differs from what the student experiences. Life looks different from the back of the room, which is why student input is so valuable. Respectful environments can be created through many strategies: class meetings, sharing times, discussions about language, friendship, responsibility, and of course, bullying. Some strategies work across age/ability levels, some will be more age/ability specific, but I have found that even the youngest children have something to say about how their classroom should feel. One kindergarten principal told me that their building held to the rule, "We don't hurt anyone's insides or outsides." Five-year-olds understand that.

One fifth-grade teacher, whose class I visited, talked with her students about "what respect looks like." She used students' answers to create a graphic organizer on a large sheet of paper. The next week she asked the class, "What does bullying look like?" and they made another graphic organizer. The two hung side by side on the bulletin board. The read-aloud book was *Racing the Past* by Sis Deans,[2] about a fifth grade boy who is bullied by another boy on the school bus. After discussing the book, the students looked at the behaviors that they had previously listed, and they were proud to see how much they knew.

My sophomores created a map/graphic organizer to define bullying and identify bullying behaviors. I put their comments on the board, and they copied them into their notebooks. That provided the introduction

to *Out of Control*, a novel by Norma Fox Mazer[3] that deals with bull y-
ing and sexual harassment. Told in the first-person voices of one of the
bullies, Rollo, and the target, Valerie, Mazer's novel enables us to hear
their thoughts about the incident. My students could identify with the
confusion Rollo faced in accepting that the fun had gotten out of control. They also realized that the harassment had seriously and deeply
violated Valerie. During the discussion of the book, several students
pointed to our Acceptance Poster for support of respectful behavior.

Teacher Behaviors

Here are a couple of do's and don't's that I can best illustrate by telling
a story. A female student came to me for help. In one of her classes, a
male student who sat behind her would reach between her arms and her
body to place his hands on her breasts. She would tell him to stop, but
he would just say something like, "You know you like it!" One day
when the teacher turned around from the board, the male quickly
slipped his hands back and placed them on the young woman's shoulders, pretending to give her a massage. The teacher, having only seen
the student's hands on the young woman's shoulders, told him to stop
it. The male student said, "But she likes it." The teacher then asked the
female student if it bothered her. She was embarrassed and said, "It's
okay, I guess." The teacher let it drop.

First the Don't's:

- Don't ask a target in front of the harasser and an audience if she or
  he is being harassed. The public pressure dictates her/his answer.
- Don't let the behavior continue, after you notice it the first time, no
  matter what either person says.

Now the Do's:

- Do remember that you are the adult in charge. If this behavior is
  inappropriate in your classroom, it must stop. Even if the two students were husband and wife, a neck massage, not to mention
  groping, would still be inappropriate in science or math or English
  or any other classroom.
- Do something! The easiest solution here would be to change students' seat assignments. I would move that young man to the front
  seat, where I could keep an eye on him. If he kept moving around

the room, ignoring my instructions, always to sit behind a female student, further steps would be taken. At times I have asked a male staff member to talk with a male student about respectful behavior toward women.

A teacher can only react to the behavior he or she sees, but as the adult in charge, the teacher needs to confront that behavior. What message did the teacher convey by letting the male student (in the above example) define what is appropriate in that classroom?

A quick and easy technique that crosses from the classroom to the hallways is called "Name It, Claim It, Stop It." I don't remember where I first heard about this strategy, but I have since found it on the GLSEN web site.[4] In the hallway or in the cafeteria, I have heard or seen disr e-spectful behavior, often bullying behaviors. If I hadn't known the students involved, I sometimes handled it poorly, either by walking away or by charging in and asking names, thereby putting the students in the position of power and admitting my disadvantage. Teacher nightmares of chasing students down hallways, outdoors, and into parking lots in an attempt to confirm an identity are based in reality. Too often defenses and stories of what may have happened complicate the situation. "Name It, Claim It, Stop It" allows me to remain calm, objective, and in charge. No one wants a public showdown, where the target will be embarrassed, the harasser will get into trouble, and I will be late for class or lunch or say something I wouldn't if I had kept a cool head.

Here's one example: I was racing to my study hall duty from my classroom on another floor a minute or two late. A female student was coming down the other side of the hall. She went to her classroom and discovered the door was closed and locked. She announced, "Damn, the fucking bitch locked me out!" I heard it, the other students in the hall heard it, and they knew that I had heard it. To do nothing would have implied I condoned that behavior. I approached the student. "Miss, I heard you say, 'Damn, the fucking bitch locked me out!' (Name It) I find that disrespectful and inappropriate for a public place. (Claim It) Such language needs to stop (Stop It)." When I have used this strategy, the student has usually apologized or admitted she was wrong. Sometimes further consequences are called for, but I find this method to be a highly effective defusing strategy. The inappropriate behavior has been called to the individual's attention, I have acted calmly and objectively, and the other students have witnessed that something was done. This is probably the simplest strategy I have learned in thirty years of teaching.

It's so simple most people will forget to use it. (Is this a good place to beg? Please try this one.)

The School Building

As your classroom anti-bullying program grows, it will attract attention. Students will mention it in other classes; parents will comment on it to you, to their son or daughter's counselor, to the administration, to other parents. This observance will be good and bad. Good because it's free advertising for something you believe in. Bad because you will be called on in many new ways and may even find yourself to be the building authority. Get a committee started as soon as possible. The broader the base of support, the more shared the responsibility and the more likely a building program can be established. In forming the committee, look for diversity in as many ways as possible: teachers in the beginning, middle, and end of their teaching careers; both genders; all cultures possible; all the different subject areas, grade levels, and ability levels; and counselors, the nurse, support staff—particularly playground monitors, bus drivers, and hallway and cafeteria monitors.

Administrator involvement is crucial. Any plan you create will need their official approval to be put into action—so involve your administrator from the beginning. It will allow them to publicly share in the ownership, development, and accountability of an anti-bullying program. Politically, it is mutually beneficial, as well as practical. A building administrator can run interference for the committee, be aware of potential obstacles and budget concerns, and bring credibility to the committee's objectives.

After the committee has established itself, involving students and parents is beneficial. Again, strive for diversity. Set short- and long-term goals. Your group will know best what your building needs, and there are many resources available to guide you. For short-term goals, consider some of the following:

- Educate yourself about bullying in your building. Most teachers, when they think about it, know where it happens in the building or in the extended school environment. A survey of the staff and the students will provide more information.
- Plan an awareness training for the staff.
- Create a building set of behavior guidelines. Some schools use key words (e.g., the Respect Pledge, the Acceptance Poster). Post these guidelines throughout the building; don't overlook offices, locker rooms, school buses, and any place where students can go.

- Establish a system for reporting incidents of bullying/harassment and publicize it. Ensure that adults of both genders and not just administrators receive the reports. Sometimes students are intimidated by the title, and they believe that once the principal is involved the legalities change. Don't forget the school nurse and the librarian.
- Find helpful resources for both the target and the bully.
- Establish consequences for the bully that do more than punish: anger management classes, empathy training, community service, communication skills training, appropriate counseling.
- Educate the rest of the student population who witness bullying but do not know what to do or how to stop it.
- Recognize all existing programs and school activities that support your anti-bullying program's goals.
- Remember to involve students who are not usually in the upper echelon.

Long-term goals must be set by your committee based on factors specific to each building.

The School District

At a state training program a few years ago, I heard a knowledgeable team speak on the problems of bullying in our schools. When the time came for questions, the first person spoke to what was in all our minds: "How much do you cost? How much time do you need? And when are you available to speak in my district?" The answer stunned us. "If you can promise us that your district is serious about taking this on and that administrators will be on the task force and financially back it, we will answer those questions." We had hoped there would be an easier way. Only the newest of us in the profession (bless them) believe that teachers can do it all. The reality is, the broader the involvement—K–12, certified, noncertified, administrative, community—the more likely the chance of success.

Changing behaviors that have been accepted for generations is a huge task. Outside experts are valuable for educating the staff, but they go home. Without a willing group of people in place to continue the work, there is little chance this huge task can be accomplished. The people who live in the environment must be the ones who change it.

Cautions

The biggest obstacle to anti-bullying programs is adult attitudes. Some of your staff members will probably be bullies—though, they would never admit that. They will tell you that their style gets results. Some adult bullies take on the role of controller. Others will believe the myths, "A little bullying will help a kid toughen up!" or "Bullying is a normal part of growing up." These are no more true than the myth that the moon is made of green cheese. Research has proven all to be false. Bullying injures all parties: the angry bully who manipulates through power, the victim who hides and fears school, and the witnesses who keep silent when they know what is right. The loss of potential to this world can only be imagined.

The other staff obstacle comes from adults who model bullying behaviors and think that they are doing so for the benefit of their students. I have heard teachers call students "Lard Butt," "Dummy," "Sexy," or similar names in front of other students and believe that they were being helpful. I heard another teacher tell a student to "Sit down, you're acting like a homosexual!" The student dropped the class that day with his parents' full support. One teacher used the word "whigger," trying to be "with it" and ended up in the principal's office.

But teachers do not just use words to bully. A friend of mine told me that at her high school the baseball coach made each player push a peanut around the bases with his nose. What skill did that coach teach? How could such a humiliating power play be justified?

There have always been teachers who have developed their discipline skills around bullying. It is easy to resort to this, and even pretend we don't do it. But such behaviors can't make our profession proud.

What else can teachers do? If you haven't guessed yet—it's look at your own behavior. The vast majority of us do our daily best to treat young people with respect and encouragement. Teachers are human too, and we all have our own histories, language, and hang-ups. Each of us grew up experiencing bullying on some level, either as a target or a bully or a witness. We called people names, got called names, and heard others call people names. It takes some introspective thinking to sort out what we truly want to carry into our classrooms each day. It is difficult to raise our students' consciousness and not our own.

The last word of caution I have is, don't try to get everyone on board. It will never happen, and it doesn't need to happen. A very effective program can be created and set up without 100 percent involvement of the school community. Some staff have very good reasons for not being involved, and some have no reasons whatsoever, but don't put your focus there. Work with the ones willing to sign on, and you will be surprised who joins the second year, or who stops you in the hall to ask for your help.

In the chapters that follow I have provided titles and descriptions of books that contain bullies. They range from primary picture books to sophisticated high school novels. Ten books in each chapter have an in-depth summary, activities, topics for discussion, and quotes for reader response. Some of the picture books can be paired with older level books or could be used to introduce the topic to students at any grade level, generate discussion in a counseling group, or involve adults in a staff or community meeting. Included are some very well-written non-fiction titles that seem to cross the usual grade-level boundaries.

Using these titles to talk about the problem of bullying keeps the topic on neutral ground. If the discussion follows an incident in class, those involved get the full defensive spotlight. Few will listen with open minds, and everyone has taken a side. The best time to have an open discussion with students who are receptive to objectively looking at bullying behaviors and aftereffects is before you have to discipline someone. If we want children to know how to act appropriately on the playground, we need to teach that respectful behavior early. We don't wait until the whole schoolyard has targeted a child. Expect respect, but make the expectation known while the lines of communication are open.

Like it or not, we are more than teachers. For some students we are the only healthy adult role models in their young lives. Along with teaching the established curricula, we have a primary responsibility to keep students safe, and part of that safety involves the teaching of some survival skills. Once our awareness about bullying has been raised, we can help students to deal with the problem instead of hide from it. There will probably never be a course solely focused on harassment and bullying, except maybe in sociology, and I don't think there should be. But literature can be used to teach many of the skills we would be teaching anyway while we address the problem of bullying.

With their enthusiasm and creativity, elementary teachers will find many ways to integrate these books with their class work. I don't worry about them because they are very involved in building a sense of community and appropriate behavior. Plus the students who are targeted are not yet very skilled in hiding their hurt. Teachers at these early grade levels are involved in most parts of their students' lives.

Often in secondary schools, the facts come first. The classics must be taught, the lectures delivered. However, language arts and English teachers can use these "bully" books in a number of ways that will complement the established lessons. These titles could be paired with required books/classics; assigned in book circles (literature circles); suggested for reading workshops and independent reading; considered for summer reading; or presented in themed units on alienation, prejudice and discrimination, choices and consequences, civic responsibility, communication, social justice, social consciousness, morality, integrity, tolerance, or peer pressure. There are enough titles listed in the following chapters to give each student a different book. Dialogue groups could be formed around commonalties. Librarians will hopefully order new titles from the annotated bibliographies at the end of each chapter, making these books available to the young people who haunt the safety of the library and need to find them. Counselors might read passages to stimulate discussion in support groups. Teachers could form their own reading groups with other teachers.

New titles keep coming, so of course this list is not complete. I apologize for omitting any titles that are favorites, but I tried to focus on books that are still in print and were published after 1990. Any recommendations are welcomed.

I truly believe that most teachers who ignore bullying behaviors do so because they do not know how to respond. I want *The Bully in the Book and the Classroom* to be a resource tool for teachers. By educating ourselves and working through stories that engage our students in discussions, we have a way to do something. To do nothing is no longer an option; too much is at stake.

Notes

1. James Howe, *The Misfits.* (New York: Simon & Schuster, 2001).
2. Sis Deans, *Racing the Past.* (New York: Henry Holt and Company, 2001).
3. Norma Fox Mazer, *Out of Control.* (New York: Avon Books, 1993).
4. WWW.GLSEN.ORG GLSEN is the Gay, Lesbian, Straight Education Network.

Chapter Three

Starting Early to Build a Respectful Environment, K–3 Grade

Whenever I have asked elementary teachers to list bullying behaviors, the first one mentioned is name-calling. Children feel powerful when they call someone an unkind name. Most little ones start with "STUPID!" I have seen high school students react more explosively to that word than swear words. There is strength in the short comeback, and it is a quick face-saving attempt. Personally I think the names change with the age, but the behaviors and need to hurt do not, whether the one shouting the name is 4, 14, 34, or 54. When we confront a student who has called someone a name, perhaps we should counsel from the wise perspective of someone who admits to still using that behavior. Words hurt. We count on them to hurt, and when we tell a student that words don't hurt, we make ourselves look foolish.

This age is the right time to start teaching the need for respect, for others and for self. Most young students know and will tell us the right way to treat people. They do need reminders, as do many adults. They are entering a new environment and learning new structures, systems, skills, and responses. They are also developing friendships. How to be a good friend is a skill needed for life. What better time to introduce or reinforce the need for respectful treatment of others and for oneself?

Because this chapter covers such a wide range of reading levels, I have started with picture books. Many of these can be used with older students to begin a bully unit.

Picture Books

Martine Agassi,
Hands Are not for Hitting.
Marieka Heinlen, Illustrator.
Nonfiction.

Hands are used for many things, like waving good-bye, shaking hands, and drawing pictures. There is a whole language, sign language, used by hands. Hands help us to play sports and dress ourselves and pet puppies. But hands can also hurt. There are other ways to deal with the feelings that make hands hit people. That is not what hands are for. At the back of the book there are activities and references listed.

Activities/Topics for Discussion

- Look at all the hands in the classroom. How are they alike? How are they different?
- Can anyone's hands do special tricks? Share them.
- Make a list of all the good things hands can do to help you or others.
- Instead of hitting someone, what is one thing you could do to release negative feelings?
- Make a big Pledge Poster that says, "Hands Are Not For Hitting." Everyone who agrees and wants to sign the pledge can use washable paint and leave his/her handprint on the poster. Hang the Pledge Poster where everyone can see it.
- Do you ever use your hands to help you tell a story? Demonstrate.

Quotations for Reader Response

- Hands are for helping.
- It's not okay for grown-ups to hit, either.
- Hands are for being kind and showing love.

Patty Lovell, *Stand Tall, Molly Lou Melon*. David Catrow, Illustrator.

Molly Lou Melon, a very short first grader, has the spirit of ten kids twice her size. Besides being tiny, she has buckteeth, a bullfrog voice, and a tendency to be clumsy. But her grandmother's wise advice helps Molly Lou shine, even when she moves to a new school and has to prove herself to the class bully, Ronald Durkin.

Activities/Topics for Discussion

- How does Molly Lou Melon feel about herself?
- What do you think of the grandmother's advice?
- At her new school, how did the other children treat Molly Lou? How did Ronald Durkin treat her?
- Why didn't Molly Lou Melon get angry at Ronald Durkin?
- How did Ronald Durkin change after he met Molly Lou Melon?
- Molly Lou Melon was so tiny that she had to use a ladder to climb into bed. Her grandmother told her to walk proudly. Discuss and demonstrate how body language shows how you feel inside. Practice walking proudly.
- Write a letter to Molly Lou Melon from her grandmother, or to Ronald Durkin from Molly Lou Melon. Give at least one sentence of advice in your letter.
- Ronald Durkin called Molly Lou Melon names. Make a list of hurtful names the class has heard used. Discuss how being called a name makes a person feel. Make a list of positive things to say to other students. (Keep this list posted in the classroom and add to it over time.)

Quotes for Discussion

- "Believe in yourself and the world will believe in you too."

- All the children cried with joy to be free of Ronald Durkin for the rest of the afternoon and Ronald Durkin felt very foolish.
- "Dear Grandmother. I wanted to tell you that everything you told me was exactly right!"

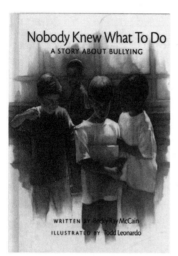

Becky Ray McCain, *Nobody Knew What to Do: A Story About Bullying.* Todd Leonardo, Illustrator.

Written from the bystander's perspective, this book taps into the helpless feeling we can all identify with when we see someone being victimized. Ray was being picked on at school. Other students saw it happen but did not know what to do. They tried ignoring the mean words in hopes that Ray would solve the problem himself. They tried sticking together, but the bullies pulled Ray out. The bystanders started to feel ashamed of their silence. When the boy telling the story hears the bullies planning their next attack, he knows he has to do something, and he goes to his teacher. The next day on the playground when the bullies start their bullying, the teacher and the principal appear and deal with the problem. This picture book is beautifully illustrated and multicultural.

Activities/Topics for Discussion

- What does bullying look like in this book? How did the bullies behave toward Ray?
- What does bullying look like in your school?
- Why did the boys pick on Ray? Was that a good reason to pick on someone?
- In this book, where did the bullying happen? Why might bullying happen in those places?

- At your school, where does bullying happen? Why does it happen in those places?
- If you saw someone picked on, what would you do?
- What do you think everyone in your building needs to do to stop bullying?

Quotes for Reader Response

- Nobody likes to think about it.
- Ray was trying hard to be brave.
- That's when I knew I had to do something.
- Together we know what to do and say.

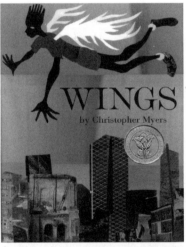

Christopher Myers, *Wings.*

Ikarus Jackson, the new kid on the block, has trouble being accepted at school because he is different. He has wings, "long, strong, proud wings." But the other students call him "Flyboy" and whisper and stare. Only one quiet, timid girl thinks his wings are beautiful, but she can't confront them, the same ones who make fun of her. Later as she watches their laughter make Ikarus fall from the sky, she finds her voice and her courage to stop their harassment and tells Ikarus his flying is beautiful. She has a new friend.

Activities/Topics for Discussion

- Why does the girl in the story understand how Ikarus feels?
- How did the teacher treat Ikarus? Brainstorm other things the teacher could have done.

- Having wings would certainly change your life. Make a chart of the positive ways and the negative ways your life would be different if you had wings like Ikarus.
- The bullies pick on Ikarus because of his wings. They act like having the wings is a bad thing, but they really are very beautiful and let Ikarus fly. Can you think of other things that some people think are bad or ugly but are really good or beautiful?

Quotes for Reader Response

- Their words sent Ikarus drifting
  Into the sky, away
  From the glaring eyes
  And the pointing fingers.
  I waited for them
  To point back at me
- I knew how he felt, how lonely
  He must be. Maybe I
  Should have said something
  To those mean kids.
- I told him
  What someone should have long ago:
  "Your flying is beautiful."

Alexis O'Neill. *The Recess Queen* Laura Huliske-Beith, Illustrator.

Mean Jean, "the Recess Queen," rules the playground at every recess and she isn't nice about it. When teeny-tiny Katie Sue moves into town she doesn't know that Mean Jean controls all. Katie Sue's love of playing challenges Mean Jean and her rules. After Katie Sue talks back to Mean Jean, she pulls out a jump rope and asks Jean to play.

Activities/Topics for Discussion

- Have you ever seen people like Mean Jean on the playground? How do you handle a recess queen or king?
- How do the other students in the book feel about Mean Jean? How do the pictures show this?
- How did Katie Sue change Mean Jean?
- Recess time has been changed. How is it better?
- Complete a Venn diagram of how the playground was at the beginning of the book compared to how it was at the end of the book.
- Katie Sue made up a rhyme to get Mean Jean to jump rope with her. Make up a rhyme that tells how to be a friend.
- Write a journal entry for the day Katie Sue came to school. Pretend to be either Katie Sue or Mean Jean. Describe what happened on the playground. How would their entries be different? Discuss them.
- Make a list of ways you can help a new student have a nice time at your school.

Quotes for Reader Response

- Here's one thing true—until that day no one DARED ask Mean Jean to play.
- "Katie Sue! A teeny kid. A tiny kid. A kid you might scare with a jump and a 'Boo!'"
- Then from the side a kid called out, "Go, Jean, Go!" And too surprised to even shout, Jean jumped in with Katie Sue.
- Bouncity, kickity, swingity,
  Hoppity, skippity, jumpity
  Ringity, zingity, YESSSSSS!

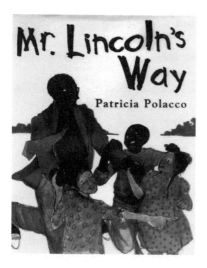

Patricia Polacco, *Mr. Lincoln's Way.*

Fifth grader Mean Gene has an abundance of anger. He calls people names and is mean to those different from him. Mr. Lincoln, a loved and respected principal, sees a way to connect with Mean Gene through Gene's love of birds, and he asks Gene to help in creating a natural environment in the school's atrium. This positive project helps Gene to change.

Activities/Topics for Discussion

- What was Mr. Lincoln's attitude toward his students? Toward Gene?
- What had Gene learned from his father? From his grandfather?
- What is an atrium? Why did Gene like working on the atrium?
- How did Gene change during the book?
- Why did Mr. Lincoln compare the children of the school to the birds?
- Complete a three bubble-graphic organizer that compares and contrasts the characteristics of Mr. Lincoln, Gene's father, and Gene's grandfather.
- Mr. Lincoln was very good at using Eugene's interest to help him overcome an intolerance of differences. Write another chapter where another student learns this same valuable lesson.
- Make a "Wanted" poster for either a principal, a teacher, or a student. Identify and list the five best qualities needed for the person in the poster. Explain your poster to the class.
- Identify two kinds of people or animals in the story that were coaxed into trusting. Why was it hard for them to trust? How were they changed because they did that?

Questions for Reader Response

- "Mean Gene" is what everybody called him. Mean Gene sassed the teachers and beat up on most of the other kids on the playground.
- "He's not a bad boy, really," Mr. Lincoln said. "Only troubled."
- "You'll think of something, Eugene. I know you will," Mr. Lincoln said. And he put his hand on Eugene's shoulder.
- "He [Gene] singled out two of our students from Mexico—he called them brown-skinned toads, and other unacceptable names."
- "My old man calls you real bad names, Mr. Lincoln. He's got an ugly name for just about everybody that's different from us."

Annotated Bibliography

Picture Books
Some books are also appropriate for other levels. I- Intermediate; M- Middle School

Agassi, Martine. Illustrated by Marieka Heinlen. *Hands Are Not for Hitting*. Minneapolis: Free Spirit, 2001. This picture book shows the many good things hands can do. (I)

Berenstain, Stan & Jan. *The Berenstain Bears and the Bully*. New York: Random House, 1993. Sister Berenstain gets beat up by a bully named Tuffy. When Brother finds out Tuffy is a girl, he teaches Sister to fight for herself. When she does, she and Tuffy end up in the principal's office.

Best, Carl. Illustrated by Giselle Potter. *Shrinking Violet*. New York: Farrar, Straus & Giroux, 2001. Violet is very shy and hates to be noticed; Irvin wants to be noticed and makes fun of other people, particularly Violet. The class play helps even out their behaviors.

Bruchac, Joseph & James Bruchac. Illustrated by Jose Aruego & Ariane Dewey. *Turtle's Race with Beaver*. New York: Dial Books for Young Readers, 2003. In this retold Seneca story, Beaver refuses to share the pond with Turtle. Ownership will be decided in a swimming race.

Caple, Kathy. *The Wimp*. Boston: Houghton Mifflin, 1994. Clyde and Watson enjoy picking on Arnold, and when his older sister Rose tries to help, she becomes a target too. Arnold sees a chance to trap the bullies in their own tricks.

Christelow, Eileen. *Jerome Camps Out*. New York: Clarion Books, 1998. Jerome and his friend P. J. go to the Swamp School camping weekend and get assigned to a tent with Buster, a bully who likes to torment them. (I)

Collicott, Sharleen. *Toestomper and the Caterpillars*. Boston: Houghton Mifflin, 1999. Toestomper hangs with a mean, rude crowd until he starts caring for a bunch of caterpillars whose house he had destroyed.

Durant, Alan. Illustrated by Guy Parker-Rees. *Big Bad Bunny*. New York: Dutton Children's Books, 2001. Big Bad Bunny is on his way to town to hold up the bank; on his way he steals from everyone he meets. The banker helps Big Bad reform.

DePaola, Tomie. *Trouble in the Barkers' Class*. New York: G. P. Putnam's Sons, 2003. A new student named Carole Anne joins Morgie and Moffie's class at school. Carole Ann arrives angry and nasty. Morgie is the first to understand her.

Elya, Susan Middleton. Illustrated by Eric Brace. *Geez Louise*. New York: G. P. Putnam's Sons, 2003. Louise is a stinkbug with only one friend, Termite Tara. But after Louise beats Kiki the roach in an ice skating contest, she becomes a hero.

Faulkner, Matt. *Black Belt*. New York: Alfred A. Knopf, 2000. At Bushi's school, the little kids are called Guppies and the big kids are called Bullfrogs. One day as Bushi is leaving school, one of the Bullfrogs, Yag-yu, grabs him and starts embarassing him. Bushi manages to escape and hides out in a doja (karate school), where he has a magical adventure that gives him the strength to face Yag-yu. (I)

Isenberg, Barbara & Susan Wolf. Illustrated by Diane DeGroat. *Albert the Running Bear Gets the Jitters*. New York: Houghton Mifflin, 1987. Albert is a marathon running bear, but a new bear from Alaska comes to the zoo and challenges Albert. Boris doesn't always play fair, but Albert learns the RELAXercise, to calm his fears and help him win the race.

Kasza, Keiko. *The Rat and the Tiger*. New York: G. P. Putnam's Sons, 1993. Tiger and Rat are good friends now but not too long ago Tiger had unknowingly bullied Rat.

————. *The Mightiest*. New York: G. P. Putnam's Sons, 2001. A Lion, an elephant, and a bear find a crown marked "For the Mightiest" in the woods. As they fight over which of them should wear the crown, a giant bully arrives and then his tiny mother shows up.

Keats, Jack Ezra. *Goggles*. New York: Viking, 1969, reissued 1998. Archie and Peter find a pair of motorcycle goggles in an abandoned lot, but three older boys decide they want the goggles. Peter, Archie, and their dachshund, Willie, trick the bullies. (I)

Lee, Milly. Illustrated by Yangsook Choi. *Nim and the War Effort*. New York: Farrar, Straus & Giroux, 1997. Set in San Francisco's Chinatown during WWII, Nim wants to collect the most newspapers for the school paper drive to support the war effort. Garland tells Nim the drive is for the American War and only a "real" American should win the prize for collecting the most. (I)

Lorbiecki, Marybeth, Illustrated by David Diaz. *Just One Flick of a Finger*. New York: Dial Books, 1996. Set in a high school and written in rap, this book deals with guns. Jack is tired of being pushed about by Reebo, and ignoring the advice of his friend, Sherms, Jack takes the gun to school. (I/M)

Lovell, Patty. Illustrated by David Catrow. *Stand Tall, Molly Lou Melon*. New York: Putnam, 2001. Molly Lou is the tiniest child ever, but her grandmother taught her to believe in herself. When she transfers to a new school this giant-sized spirit makes friends with everyone, even the school bully.

McCain, Becky Ray. Illustrated by Todd Leonardo. *Nobody Knew What to do: A Story About Bullying*. Morton Grove, IL: Albert Whitman & Company, 2001. Ray is getting picked on at school, and a small group of kids want to help but do not know what to do. (I)

Millman, Dan. Illustrated by T. Taylor Bruce. *Secret of the Peaceful Warrior*. Tiburon, CA: H. J. Kramer, 1991. Danny and his family move to a new town. One day while trying to escape the neighborhood bully, he bumps into Socrates, an elderly neighbor who teaches him gentle ways to handle the bully. (I/M)

Modarressi, Mitra. *The Beastly Visits*. New York: Orchard Books, 1996. Newton looks like a monster, but he is really very nice. He and his family live in a burrow under Miles' house. They become playmates, and by standing up for each other, they defeat the playground bully.

Myers, Christopher. *Wings*. New York: Scholastic Press, 2000. Everyone thinks Ikarus Jackson's wings are ugly except for one quiet girl who finds her voice to tell Ikarus his wings are beautiful. (I)

Rimes, LeAnn. Illustrated by Richard Bernal. *Jag*. New York: Dutton Children's Books, 2003. On her first day of school the other young jaguars make fun of Jag's name, and when they find out she is afraid of the water, they laugh even harder. Then Jag makes a friend, a black jaguar with no spots.

Pearson, Tracey Campbell. *Myrtle*. New York: Farrar, Straus & Giroux, 2004. Myrtle has a wonderful life until mean Frances moves next door and picks on Myrtle and her little brother. Not until Aunt Tizzy visits does Myrtle learn she can make her own happiness.

Polacco, Patricia. *Mr Lincoln's Way*. New York: Philomel Books, Penguin Putnam, 2001. Mr. Lincoln is the coolest principal ever. He even has an understanding way with Eugene Esterhause, also called Mean Gene, who terrorizes the playground. Mr. Lincoln notices Eugene's interest in birds and enlists his help with filling the school's empty atrium. (I)

O'Neill, Alexis. Illustrated by Laura Huliske-Beith. *The Recess Queen*. New York: Scholastic Press, 2002. Mean Jean rules the playground until teeny-tiny Katie Sue shows up. Before she can learn Mean Jean's playground rules, Katie Sue offers friendship.

Rosenberg, Liz. Illustrated by Stephen Gammell. *Monster Mama*. New York: Philomel Books, 1993. Patrick Edward has a quiet confidence and doesn't frighten when three bullies tie him to a tree, but when they make fun of his mother he lets out such a furious scream that Monster Mama shows up and teaches the bullies a lesson in respect.

Seskin, Steve & Allen Shamblin. Illustrated by Glin Dibley. *Don't Laugh At Me*. Berkeley: Tricycle Press, 2002. The voices of many characters who are typical targets of harassment bond together to speak out in this song. (I)

Chapter Books

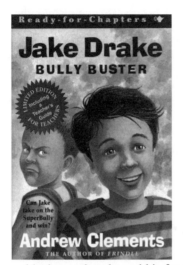

Andrew Clements, *Jake Drake Bully Buster.* Amanda Harvey, Illustrator.

Jake Drake looks back at second grade from the experienced perspective of fourth grade, because he is still using some of the things he learned then. One particularly valuable lesson taught Jake how to be a bully buster.

Jake had always been a bully magnet. He was small, not assertive, and had eyes that showed his fear. The bullies could tell Jake would be an easy target. In second grade Link Baxter, Super Bully, moved to town, and he especially liked to bully Jake. When they were assigned a class project together, Jake started to see behind Link's bully mask and found a real kid underneath.

Activities/Topics for Discussion

- When was the first time Jake was bullied? When was the first time you were bullied? Are there any similarities between you and Jake?
- Jake describes all the bullies in his past. Make a chart listing each bully and his bullying specialty. Can the class think of more bully specialties?
- Vocabulary words—*bully magnet, bullyitis, bully buster.* Can anyone act them out? Draw a picture?
- Jake doesn't want to tell any adults that he is being bullied. Sometimes you need to tell an adult if someone is bullying you. When should you tell?
- What is the difference between tattling and telling? (Tattling gets someone in trouble. Telling keeps someone safe.)

Quotations for Reader Response

- If everybody who works at school is so smart, how come they can't get rid of the bullies? How come when it comes to bullies, kids are mostly on their own? (5)
- You see, Link was no ordinary bully . . . Link Baxter, well . . . he got inside my head—and it only took him twenty minutes. No doubt about it. This was a bully with real talent. (18)
- "My name's Jake, Jake Drake." . . . now he knows that I cared about him goofing around with my name.

  Link smiled that special bully-smile. He said, "Yeah, I know. Like I said. Your name's Fake, Fake Drake." (21)
- Link had gotten into me! I was being like Link. I had caught BULLYITIS! (27)
- Abby shrugged. "If I get mad, I feel mean. I don't like to feel mean. So I don't get mad." (33)
- Maybe a bully stops being a bully if there aren't some other kids around to watch. I thought that maybe he's only a SuperBully when he has an audience. (44)
- Bullies don't fool me anymore. Because back behind those mean eyes and that bully-face, there's another face. A real face.

  And if I keep looking for that real face, I see it. And the bully sees me see it.

  And BAM, just like that, another bully gets busted. (73)

Judy Cox, *Mean, Mean Maureen Green*. Cynthia Fisher, Illustrator.

Sometimes when we are afraid of something, we have to just keep on going. Lilley is afraid of many things: learning how to ride a bike; Bruno, the fierce dog on the way to school; and Maureen Green, the baddest fourth grader, who has just been assigned to Lilley's school bus. Maureen likes to threaten people; she claims her own seat on the bus and stands at the door to Lilley's third-grade class and growls. Lilley has to find a way to avoid the bus. Adam suggests they ride their bikes to school—but Lilley can't, she's afraid. With her dad's help, she conquers her fear of riding a two-wheel bike. The first day she and Adam plan to ride to school, Lilley is late and Adam has left. Facing another fear, she rides to school alone, past the ferocious dog, down the biggest hill in town, and right through Marueen Green's blockade.

Lilley arrives at school, proud and brave. The next time she wants to ride the bus, Maureen will just have to move over.

Activities/Topics for Discussion

- What are some of the rumors about Maureen Green? Does Lilley think they are true?
- Did Maureen actually do anything to hurt anyone? How does she intimidate people?
- Do you remember being afraid to ride a bike? Or maybe there was something else you were afraid to do. Did you try? How did you feel after you faced that fear?
- How does Adam treat Maureen?
- After Lilley rides to school alone, she thinks of all the things she can do: ride a bike, do thirty chin-ups, and stand up to Maureen

Green. She feels strong. Make a list of all the things you can do. Everything counts; nothing is unimportant.

Quotes for Reader Response

- Lilley curled up against the window. If only she could turn into a mouse. If only Maureen wouldn't see her. (5)
- "Listen up!" she [Maureen] yelled. The noisy bus was suddenly silent.

   Her voice echoed. "From now one, the backseat is my seat! I own this seat!" (7)
- Lilley's eyes widened. "Dad! Maureen doesn't make friends. She takes prisoners!" (13)
- Lilley sneaked a peek at the backseat. Maureen saw her. She raised her right hand, and very slowly curled each finger into a fist. She shook it right at Lilley. Lilley shivered. (19)
- What kind of a bully wears pink bunnies? Why, Maureen's just a bossy fourth-grader with chicken pox! I had chicken pox when I was three. And pink bunnies! I wear pink bunnies, thought Lilley. And I'm a wimp! (77)
- I'm free! I can fly! I can ride a bike. I can do thirty chin-ups. I can conquer a bully!

   "I'm Tiger Lilley!" (79)

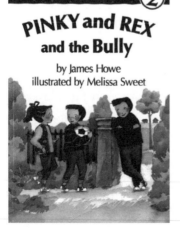

READY-TO-READ ②
PINKY and REX and the Bully
by James Howe
illustrated by Melissa Sweet

James Howe, *Pinky and Rex and the Bully.* Melissa Sweet, Illustrator.

Pinky loves the color pink, so he uses his nickname instead of his real name, William. His best friend is a girl named Rex. But then Kevin, the third-grade bully, decides only a girl would be named Pinky. Now, Pinky starts to wonder if he should change his name.

Activities/Topics for discussion

- How are Pinky and Rex alike? How are they different?
- Make a list of all the things Kevin does to embarrass Pinky.
- What did Pinky do to change his personality/identity?
- How did Pinky stand up to the bully? Brainstorm a list of things you could do if a bully bothers you.
- Ask students to role play the following scenes and share how each person felt.
  - Pages 1–5. Kevin knocks Pinky off his bike, and Mrs. Morgan intervenes.
  - Pages 13–16. At recess, Kevin and friends begin to pick on Pinky. Anthony confronts Kevin.
  - Pages 18–23. Pinky decides to change his name and give away his stuffed animals.
- Make a chart. On one side list things boys usually like to do. On the other side, list things girls like to do. Look at both lists. Could boys and girls both do all the things?

Quotes for Discussion

- "You're a sissy, Pinky!" the boy shouted. "Get up and fight."
  Pinky lay on the sidewalk where the third-grader had knocked him off his bike. His cheeks were fever-hot. (1)
- "I was trying to help him up," Kevin lied. He pretended to pat Pinky on the shoulder, but pinched him hard instead. (3)
- His favorite color was what had gotten him into trouble with the bully. (8)
- "Because I don't like pink." Pinky told her. "And a boy shouldn't have a pink bike. And Pinky is a dumb name for a boy. And a boy shouldn't play with girls." (28)
- "Don't change for other people, Billy [Pinky]. Other people will come and go in your life. Do what's right for the one person who will always be with you—yourself." (32)

Marisa Montes, *Get Ready for Gabí #2, Who's that Girl?* Joe Cepeda, Illustrator.

Maritza Gabriela Morales Mercado, also known as Gabí the Great, may only be in third grade, but she wants to be a crime fighter. Her red cowgirl boots and red beach towel cape help her in the fight against bullying.

As she and Miguelito, her four-year-old brother, walk through their neighborhood, they notice a moving van in front of the old haunted house. Their hopes swell. Maybe a family with children will move in. Shortly after, Gabí meets Lizzie, the new neighbor. Gabí and her two friends, Devin and Jasmine, visit and the four girls become friends. Unfortunately, Gabí soon realizes that the twin boys who have been terrorizing her little brother are Lizzie's older brothers. Lizzie refuses to believe that her brothers could be so mean. When Gabí stands up for Miguelito, the boys laugh at her and make fun of her Spanish. She wants to keep Lizzie for a friend, but these bullies make it very difficult, until they give themselves away. Lizzie steps in and tells her brothers to apologize.

In Gabí's home they speak Spanish all the time because her mother's family is from Puerto Rico. There are many Spanish words and phrases used in the telling of the story; a glossary at the back provides readers with English equivalents.

Activities/Topics for Discussion

- From the beginning of the story, Devin seems to be concerned about something. What is bothering her and how is the problem solved?
- How are Gabí and Lizzie alike? Make a chart showing all the characteristics they share.
- List the things the bully twins do to harass other kids.

- Gabí, her family, and Devin can all speak Spanish. Try to learn a few of the Spanish words used in the story. Who in your class can speak another language besides English? Practice saying hello in other languages.
- Write a letter to the bully twins that Miguelito might have written.
- How does Lizzie feel about her leg brace? How might she have been teased about her leg?

Quotes for Reader Response

- "They were mean. They said, 'Little kids have to pay a toll.' Then they wouldn't let me pass. And then, I cried. And then . . . they laughed at me!" (39)
- I was aching to fix those bullies, but I knew I had to calm down. (41)
- First Bully: "Little kids can't—"
  Second Bully: "—go past this line."
  They pointed at a crack in the sidewalk. (44)
- "You'd better stop picking on my brother!"
  The Twins looked at each other for a second and totally cracked up. Then they started stomping their feet and doing a tap dance on the sidewalk. It was like they had planned it ahead of time. (47)
- "Jack and Jake are my brothers. They would never be mean to anybody. Ever!"
  My eyes slid over to the chunky twins who stood behind her. They smirked. They waved their fingers. Then they winked at me. (73)
- "If you really want to be her friend [Lizzie's], you won't give up on her. She loves her brothers, and she was doing what she thought was right." (80)
- The twins went back and forth, talking gibberish. It took a few moments before I got it. They were making fun of my Spanish! (85)
- "You guys *are* bullies." She [Lizzie] walked toward her brothers. "Now you've made me lose the only neighborhood friend I've ever had. I wouldn't blame Gabí if she never talked to me again." (88)

What could be worse than the class bully?

Laurence Yep,
Cockroach Cooties.

Nine-year-old Teddy likes to stay out of harm's way, but his younger brother Bobby can't seem to avoid trouble, particularly when the school bully, Arnie-zilla, starts harassing him. Teddy feels a duty to protect Bobby from Arnie. But after Teddy has used up most of his tricks, Bobby comes to the rescue with a cockroach named Hercules, which terrifies Arnie. It's this fear that provides some insight into Arnie's lonely home life. His mom works two jobs and doesn't have time to clean the apartment, so he sometimes wakes up with cockroaches crawling on his bed. His father left a long time ago. The only way Arnie knows how to survive is to be tough.

Set in and around Chinatown in San Francisco, this book shows that bullying can exist anywhere. It also provides some glimpses into the Chinese-American culture.

Activities/Topics for Discussion

- Does it surprise you that bullying exists in a private school run by nuns? In an all Chinese environment?
- Why was Arnie a bully? Did Bobby's trick make Arnie stop being a bully? Why?
- By the end of the book, what do we know about Arnie's life that contributes to his being a bully?
- Teddy and Bobby are brothers who look out for each other, but what clues are given that prove Teddy has bullied Bobby in the past?
- At the restaurant, how does Teddy and Bobby's father bully the waiters?
- Make a chart of Bobby's and Teddy's and Arnie's fears. List each character's fears under his name.

Quotes for Reader Response

- "There are two kinds of people in this world—the bullies and the victims. Guess which bunch we belong to?"
  "But why does it have to be that way?" (22)
- To everyone's amazement, he [Arnie] said, "He was in the Ming Dynasty." It was the only time I saw him smile without making someone else cry. (31)
- Suddenly I went flying through the air. Everyone laughed again when I landed. As I sat up, Arnie drew his foot in.
  "Later." He grinned wickedly. Arnie-zilla was back. (32)
- When Bobby got pigheaded, I usually bounced him around a little. He always came to his senses after that. But I was being just like Arnie again. (104)
- Arnie grinned wickedly. "Today, I've got a special deal. Two beatings for the price of one." (116)
- As a bully, Arnie was a real artist. Your average bully would just start hitting you. However, that wasn't enough for Arnie. He wanted to prolong the humiliation. (117)
- If I grew up on my own, I guess I'd have to be pretty tough, too. I might even turn out like Arnie. (126)
- Arnie ignored the attention though. He'd been getting into trouble ever since he had come to school. I guess he didn't care what people thought—so long as they thought he was tough. (129)

Annotated Bibliography
Some books may be used at other levels. I-Intermediate students

Bates, Betsy. Illustrated by Leslie Morrill. *Tough Beans*. New York: Holiday House, 1988. Nat Berger has diabetes, and suddenly he has to learn new rules—what to eat, how to give himself shots, and how to deal with Jasper Denletter, the new bully in town. (I)

Berenstain, Stan & Jan. *The Bernstain Bears and the Bully*. New York: Random House, 1993. Sister Bear gets beat up by Tuffy, a girl bully at school. Brother Bear teaches Sister some defensive boxing. The next week Sister stops Tuffy from throwing rocks at birds and after a tussle, both are sent to the principal.

Caseley, Judith. *Bully.* New York: Greenwillow Books, 2001. Mickey's ex-friend Jack has turned into a bully and steals Mickey's cookies and breaks his pencils. Mickey tries many different things to find the Jack who used to be his friend.

Clements, Andrew. *Jake Drake, Bully Buster.* New York: Aladdin Paperbacks, 2001. Until second grade, Jake Drake was the perfect target for bullies—kind of small, kind of smart, and with no older brother to take care of him. From the wisdom of fourth grade, Jake looks back on how he turned into a bully buster. (I)

Crisp, Marty. Illustrated by True Kelly. *My Dog, Cat.* New York: Holiday House, 2000. Abbott Williamson III, known as Abbie, wants a big dog named Killer to protect him from Pete Street, the fourth- grade bully. But what Abbie gets is his aunt's Yorkshire terrier named Cat while she vacations. Cat has enough attitude to take on the world and Pete Street. (I)

Cox, Judy. Illustrated by Cynthia Fisher. *Mean, Mean Maureen Green.* New York: Holiday House, 1999. Third-grader Lilley learns to face her fears. She escapes a mean dog, learns to ride her bike, and faces down the fourth grade bully, Maureen Green. (I)

Dale, Jenny. *Billy the Brave Puppy.* New York: Aladdin, 2000. Martin gets a puppy, Billy, who is afraid of everything. When Billy sees Jamie Jones threatening Martin, he finds his growl. Martin learns to be as brave as his puppy.

Davis, Gibb. Illustrated by Abby Carter. *Camp Sink or Swim.* New York: Random House, 1997. Since Danny is almost nine years old, his parents have decided to let him go to Camp Kickapoo for the summer with his best friend Billy. Even though Danny is excited, he realizes the other kids, particularly the bully Tonya, will find out his stories about being a champion swimmer are lies. A liar and a bully learn a lot about friendship.

Duffy, Betsy. *Alien for Rent.* New York: Delacorte Press, 1999. Third graders, J. P. and Lexie have made an amazing discovery—a cute fuzzy green alien who grants wishes for Twinkies. Before Lexie realizes Bork's power, Bruce, the fifth-grade bully, has been turned into a baby. (I)

———. Illustrated by Janet Wilson. *How to be Cool in the Third Grade.* New York: Viking, 1993. Robbie York needs to know how to be cool, after all he is in third grade now. How to get his mom from taking pictures at the bus stop is just the beginning, but how to be a book buddy for Bo Haney, the class bully, may just be the end. Slowly Robbie realizes he has to ask for what he needs. (I)

Eddaugh, Susan. *Martha Walks the Dog.* New York: Houghton Mifflin, 1998. Martha, a dog, can talk. She helps Bad Dog Bob by showing that the power of nice words can change the effects of bad words.

Harvey, Jayne. Illustrated by Abby Carter. *Great Uncle Dracula.* New York: Random House, 1992. After the divorce, Emily Normal, her father, and younger brother move to Transylvania, USA to live with Great Uncle Dracula. Emily enters third grade at Transylvania elementary where her classmates are all witches, werewolves, ghosts, and vampires, and of course, a bully, who doesn't like "regular people." (I)

Hines, Anna Grossnickle. Illustrated by Karen Ritz. *Tell Me Your Best Thing.* New York: Dutton Children's Books, 1991. Sophie has had problems with Charlotte in the past, but now in third grade, Charlotte organizes a club and invites Sophie to join. To belong to the club, each girl must tell the best and the worst thing that has ever happened to her. It doesn't take long for Sophie to realize Charlotte is still the bossy bully she always was. (I)

Howe, James. Illustrated by Melissa Sweet. *Pinky and Rex and the Bully.* New York: Aladdin Paperbacks, 1996. Pinky learns that even if pink is his a favorite color and his best friend is a girl named Rex, the school bully doesn't have any right to pick on him.

Kline, Suzy. Illustrated by Frank Remkiewicz. *Horrible Harry and the Dragon War.* New York: Viking, 2002. In Miss Mackle's third-grade class, each student gets to research an animal. Harry and Song Lee pick different types of dragons, and that starts a dragon war. (I)

Kliphuis, Christine. Illustrated by Charlotte Dematons. *Robbie and Ronnie.* New York: North-South Books, 2002. Robbie and Ronnie understand that friendship is about loyalty and acceptance. Dennis and his friend don't know that and try to harass Robbie and Ronnie at the town pool. (I)

Levy, Elizabeth. Illustrated by Tim Barnes. *Third Grade Bullies.* New York: Hyperion, 1998. Sally, new to the school, tries to fit in by standing up for another girl nearly as short as she. Her defense comes out as an attack. (I)

Mead, Alice. *Junebug and the Reverend.* New York: Random House, 1998. Junebug, his mom, and his sister, Tasha, move a few weeks before the end of school. A new school, new people, new responsibilities, and a school bully all tumble into his life. Junebug learns to survive and carries a few others along with him. (I)

Romain, Trevor. *Bullies Are a Pain in the Brain*. Minneapolis, MN: Free Spirit, 1997. Nonfiction. This look at bullies and how to handle them is done with clarity, illustrations, and humor. Besides being informative, the book presents defense strategies and advice for students, school staff, and parents. (I)

Scribner, Virginia. Illustrated by Janet Wilson. *Gopher Takes Heart*. New York: Viking, 1993. Gopher Goff loses his milk money every morning on the way to school. Fletcher Simpson, the third-grade bully, takes it from him. Fletcher even bullies Gopher into giving up the class money for their teacher's Valentine. Gopher decided standing up to Fletcher and getting beat up is better than being afraid. (I)

Shipton, Jonathan. Illustrated by Claudio Munoz. *No Biting, Horrible Crocodile!* Racine, WI: Artists & Writers Guild, 1995. Flora is an unhappy little girl who wears the mask of a horrible crocodile. She goes too far and bites everyone's favorite toy, Monkey. The students help her to become a kinder, happier girl.

Soneklar, Carol. *Mighty Boy*. New York: Orchard Books, 1999. Timid and shy Howard Weinstein is "small for his age," and he hears those dreaded words far too often as he enters fourth grade at a new school. When Eddie Gervinsky calls Howard "Mighty Wimp," Howard looks to his favorite TV superhero for strength.

Williams, Karen Lynn. Illustrated by Lena Shiffman. *First Grade King*. New York: Clarion Books, 1992. Joey King is so excited to start first grade and learn to read, but then he meets Ronald Boyd, a repeater and a bully. Ronald even makes fun of Madeline because she is nearly blind. Joey's kindness and sensitivity helps everyone be nicer.

Winthrop, Elizabeth. Illustrated by Pat Grant. *Luke's Bully*. New York: Viking, 1990. Quiet and shy, third-grader Luke has to give up his lunch every day to Arthur or else! Though Luke cannot escape Arthur's reach, they slowly become friends. (I)

Wood, Brian. *The Cramp Twins: Opposites Attack*. New York: Bloomsbury Children's Books, 1995. Lucien Cramp is a daily target for his twin brother, Wayne, but at the Country and Western Barbeque, Wayne embarrasses himself.

Yep, Laurence. *Cockroach Cooties*. New York: Hyperion, 2000. Second-grader Teddy does his best to avoid Arnie, the school bully, but he can't escape when he has to defend his little brother Bobby. A cockroach comes to their rescue.

Chapter Four

Bullying and Additional Forms of Harassment Grades 4, 5, and 6

In the intermediate grades, bullying builds on behavior set in the primary grades. Name-calling, the backbone of harassment, gets upgraded with harsher synonyms for the word "stupid." Kids have learned that words carry power, and these fourth through sixth graders have discovered how to lace their put downs with sarcasm. Taunts that used to be teasing cross over into bullying. "Stupid" becomes "moron" or "idiot"; "sissy" becomes "faggot." Boys who are perceived-to-be-gay are harassed more than girls who are perceived-to-be-gay, however, "tomboy" is beginning to lose its charm. Kids who use homosexual slurs may not know what these words really mean—but they do know that those words have great power to do harm. The hurtful fists usually come later.

Sports are a bigger part of student life as physical skills develop and performance is more evaluative. The more skilled kids are playing on teams and following professional sports. The boys, particularly, want to copy their favorite sports heroes. Girls get their fashion ideas from older girls and their favorite television show or performers. When Britney Spears became popular, girls everywhere copied her style and had to have the latest "Britney" outfit.

It takes money to dress like these superstars. If a child can't afford the right shoes, sports jersey, or knit top, he/she probably won't make it very far up the school social ladder. This economic bullying only gets worse in middle school.

Girls start to form alliances, and the beginnings of girl cliques start to show. Friendships become increasingly important. Acceptance and belonging are crucial. Loneliness intensifies. They are practicing their verbal and social skills, and if there isn't anyone to practice with, one enters middle school unarmed and alone.

These years are also the make-it-or-break-it time for the bully. Bullying can be a hard habit to break because fear always works. If the bully doesn't learn alternative ways to get attention and validation and to develop the skills to make and maintain friendships, that child and what he/she could become will be lost. At this age, bullies are still frightened kids who need to learn better ways to interact than to pull power plays. If we don't help them as well as their targets, bullying will never go away. More young people will be lost, and we can't afford to lose any.

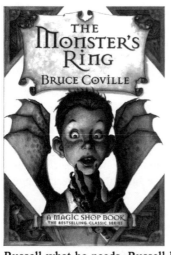

Bruce Coville, *The Monster's Ring.*

Russell Crannaker, a timid fifth grader, loves Halloween, and this year he's planned a Frankenstein costume for the school parade. He wants so badly to be scary! While he plans his costume, Eddie sneaks up behind Russell and starts threatening him. Because Eddie has already poked, punched, and smashed him on different occasions, Russell turns and runs—straight into Mr. Elives' Magic Shop. After Mr. Elives asks Russell what he needs, Russell leaves with a magical Monster's Ring. According to the directions, with one turn of the ring, Russell will turn into a monster. This can't be true, Russell thinks, but when he gets home, he decides to try it out. The ring works! One turn to the left, and he's a monster; one turn to the right, and he returns to himself. He has found the perfect costume to scare Eddie!

On Halloween day, Russell goes into the school bathroom to change into old clothes. He puts the ring on and turns it—twice—becoming a doubly terrifying monster. His horns pop out twice as long, his hair grows twice as thick all over his body and circles his head like a lion's mane, and fangs spring from his mouth and nearly touch his chest. When he speaks, his voice rumbles, snarls, growls, and roars. Russell can't wait to find Eddie.

Everyone likes Russell's costume, but Russell is starting to like the power that goes with it. The ring has not only transformed his appearance, his timid shy self has also been changed into an angry, irritable monster. He rampages down the hall and from classroom to classroom, jumping over desks, growling at teachers. Even the principal, Mr. Rafschnitz, the beast of the school, cannot stop Russell the monster.

After this incredible scene, Russell runs out of the school, hides in the bushes, and turns the ring back. Then he hears his mother's voice calling him. Timid, shy, quiet Russell crawls out of his hiding and goes to his mom.

Russell has made a discovery: As the monster, he doesn't have to be afraid; he can stand up for himself. The power of the ring calls him, tempting him to turn into a bullying monster, and he does not like that.

Later that night, under a full moon, Russell sees Eddie being dragged off by three bigger kids. Eddie is frightened and sounds like Russell does when Eddie bullies him. Russell grabs the ring on his finger and turns it three times! This time he becomes such a horrible monster, he even grows huge bat wings, his clothes burst into flames, and red metal scales cover his entire body—he becomes King of the Monsters! Flying into the night sky, amazed by his powerful wings, Russell swoops over the city until he spots Eddie and his tormentors.

After Russell deals with the bullies and sends them running, he and Eddie have a talk. Russell reveals his identity to Eddie and convinces him that future harassment on his part would not be wise.

Later as Russell tries to return to himself, he discovers there is a problem because it is the night of a full moon. A frightened Eddie helps Russell solve his problem—at least until the next full moon.

Activities/Topics for Discussion

• Russell realizes that he can become a monster anytime he wants. That makes him very happy. If you had that option, would you use it? What would you do with the ring? What would you do as a monster?

- The ring changes Russell, not just when he is wearing it and becomes the monster, but later after he has changed back. How does having been a monster change Russell even when he is back in his normal body?
- Sometimes Russell gets angry with his mother because she babies him so much. He is tired of being a wimp! Is that Russell or the monster talking?
- Russell looks at the ring and realizes that it has gotten him into a lot of trouble, but he also had a lot of fun. Why is it fun for him to get into trouble? Do you think Eddie feels the same way, that getting into trouble is fun?
- Why does Russell react so strongly when he sees three older boys terrorizing Eddie?
- After finishing the whole book, when you have the most information about them, compare and contrast Eddie and Russell.

Quotes for Reader Response

- So far that day, Eddie had poked him, punched him, called him names, and smashed him in the face with a cream-filled cupcake. Under the circumstances, only one thing made sense.
    Russell did it. He ran. (2)
- He, Russell, the meek and mild, was making tough Eddie squirm. (23)
- "If a teacher is watching, Eddie just punches me anyway and gets in trouble for the fun of it. He doesn't care what happens to him. He doesn't care what happens to anybody." (28)
- He wanted to growl and snap some more.
    He wanted to run around and howl.
    He wanted to scare the living daylights out of people! (44)
- Russell bounded off the desk. His heart was pounding, and the beast in his blood was going wild. Some of the kids screamed. Others began to edge away from him. . . . Somewhere inside him, a tiny voice was crying, *This is crazy. Crazy! Stop it. Stop it NOW!* (47)
- He hunched into himself and stared out the window. Inside he felt stronger and braver and more ready to tell people what he thought than he ever had before.
    He just didn't feel brave enough to try it on his mother. (56)
- Russell opened his mouth to take a bite out of Eddie's shoulder. That's when the warning bell went off in his head.

"What am I doing?" he cried in horror. (60)

- From the frightened expression that twisted Eddie's face, Russell could tell that he [Eddie] was feeling the same kind of fear that he, Russell, had so often felt when trapped in Eddie's grasp. (65)
- Russell, infuriated by seeing even his enemy get bullied, began to twist the ring, repeating the chant as he did. (66)
- Now that he thought about it, being plain old Russell Crannaker wasn't all that bad. (86)

Sis Deans, *Racing the Past.*

Fifth-grader Ricky Gordon makes a deal with the principal—he won't get in any more fights with the-grade six bully, Bugsie McCarthy, if Mr. Daniels won't call his mom. This means Ricky will have to go straight to his classroom in the morning, stay in during recess, and not ride the school bus, thereby eliminating all the times he and Bugsie could be in the same place at the same time. Bugsie had started the last fight announcing, "My father said the best thing your father ever did for your family was run his truck off of Dead Man's Curve." (3) Everyone heard. Ricky had to fight, even though he agreed with Bugsie. William Gordon, the victim of his own drunk driving, had been abusive to his wife and three children, and the whole town knew it. Parents kept their kids away from the Gordon children. Bugsie and his gang call Ricky and his brother Matt, "white trash." Keeping his promise to Mr. Daniels would not be easy.

Three and a half miles to school and three and a half miles home, Ricky starts walking. Every time the bus passes him, Bugsie yells insults from the back seat. In order to avoid Bugsie's harassment, Ricky has to beat the bus. So he starts jogging, and then running. Not only does he keep logs, statistics, and a journal, but his natural love for numbers also helps Ricky create number games that help him concentrate and push past the pain. Slowly the people in the town start to notice this young boy who keeps to himself, is fiercely protective of his family, works for Mr. Lewis on Saturday mornings at his mill, and is two years ahead of his class in math. The high school track coach hears about Ricky's running, and he invests in Ricky by buying him running shoes, only the second pair of new shoes Ricky has had in his whole life.

Overcoming the nightmares and trauma of years of physical and emotional abuse helps Ricky and his family to heal. His mother, a proud but beaten woman, finds strength to get her family the therapy they need. Little Matt has enough mouth to take on all the bullies on the bus, but he still fears that his father might return from the dead and come home to terrorize them again. With more responsibilities than any fifth grader should have, Ricky is more the man of the house than his father ever was. In an unusual way, Ricky's deal with the principal helps him change the reputation previously attached to the Gordon family name and bring a sense of pride back to these tightly bonded survivors.

Activities/Topics for Discussion

- Mr. Daniels, the principal, appears in only a few scenes in the book, yet we get a good idea of what kind of a principal he is. What makes him an effective or ineffective principal? Is he the kind of principal you would like? Why or why not?
- Why is *Racing the Past* a better title than *Racing the Bus*? Explain what Ricky is racing, besides the bus.
- How can a bad thing, like having to walk seven miles to get to school and back home, turn into a good thing? Who or what makes the difference?
- While Ricky runs home after school, Matt has to ride the bus. What is that ride like for Matt with Bugsie there on the bus?
- Ricky feels like he has a new mother. What was his old mother like? How has she changed?
- Why do Ricky and Matt only refer to their father as "he" or "him"?
- Lyle and Ricky are good friends—what makes their friendship so strong? Give examples of how they help each other.
- Throughout the book, Bugsie always has Norman and Dan at his side and following his orders. How do bullies like Bugsie get power over kids like Dan and Norman?
- How does Dan change by the end of the story?

- Bullies seem to be everywhere. You might not be able to get rid of them, but maybe you can change them or the situation. What are some things that Ricky did to change the situation? Create a list of directions for changing a bully into a non-bully, or a bully supporter (like Dan and Norman) into a non-supporter.
- Create a graphic organizer to compare and contrast Bugsie and Mr. Gordon, Ricky's dad.

Quotes for Reader Response

- We have to make sure your father doesn't find out, or you'll feel the back of his belt for sure. (10)
- "That's the last time he calls me Four-Eyes." (13)
- His mother on the floor trying to protect her face, his father's boots kicking at her arms, him in the middle trying to break it up, and then Matt coming out of nowhere, swinging a cast-iron fry pan. (24)
- "I've tried everything I can think of to help Matt get over those bad dreams and they're only getting worse. Waking up to those screams every night, and him wetting the bed; now he won't even go to sleep unless he has that fry pan with him." (31)
- He loved Matt so much that it'd always hurt less to take the blows when their father was on the warpath than to watch his little brother get it. (58)
- It was funny how "sorry" could change things if you meant it. (63)
- "Decisions, decisions," said Bugsie, placing a finger on his freckled chin. "Do I dunk your head in the toilet or beat your face in?" (81)
- All the day's frustration had finally caught up with him, and because there was no one there to see him, he [Ricky] let himself cry. (87)
- Ricky smiled at the memory of those cheers: *Go, Ricky, Go!* (139)
- "Check out the sneakers, guys. Where'd you steal them from, Gordon? You couldn't have found them in the church bin." (146–7)
- Everybody knows a Gordon's middle name is Thief. (147)
- Dan Simmons lingered behind. He picked up Ricky's backpack, and as he handed it to him, said, "Beat the bus, Ricky." (147–8)

Michael Laser, *6-321.*

In this memoir, Laser talks about his sixth-grade year with that gentle sense of memories, good and bad, tumbling together. There is little of today's sense of urgency; kids get beat up and they return to fight another day. Because these events happened in the sixties, looking at the bullies' behavior can be done from a safe distance. It also helps to know we can survive the events of sixth grade.

The issue of bullying exists throughout the book. Though several people bully, the two most clearly defined bullies are Nicky Raffetto, in class 6-307, and Cary Lipshitz, in Marc Chaikin's, the main character, own class of 6-321.

The two bullies operate differently. Everyone avoids Nicky Raffetto; few suspect Carl Lipshitz. Nicky fits the image and carries the reputation of the school delinquent. Big and always ready to fight, Nicky and his buddies in 6-309 like to beat up the smart but skinny guys in 6-321. Cary bullies with his words; sarcasm and clever put-downs are his weapons. He hangs with the cool, tall guys. Shortly after school begins, Nicky is moved into Mr. Vigoritti's class with Marc, Lily, and Cary. Nicky is clearly out of his element in this "smarter class," and Cary is quick to point out Nicky's inadequacies until Nicky reveals that the next time he fights, he will be expelled. He tells Cary to be ready on the last day of school. Only then does Cary start to monitor his mouth.

The most defining moment for Marc happens early in the year: he falls in love with brilliant, talented, shy Lily Wu, a friend since kindergarten. Now she fills his every thought and influences his every action, but he can't bring himself to tell her.

Cary also has an interest in Lily, and neither he nor Marc know how to handle their feelings except to compete with each other—once over a Scrabble game. However, Lily admits that she doesn't have any feelings for either of them but understands how it feels to like someone who doesn't even look your way. Lily has a crush on Nicky.

As the class prepares for its presentation of *Julius Caesar*, with Nicky playing Caesar, the boys of 6-321 can't take any more bullying from the boys in 6-309. When they set a date, time, and place for the final showdown, only Nicky and Cary think it's a crazy idea. One week later, the Friday of the fight, tempers have cooled and courage has dissipated. The boys are sitting in class, dreading the end of the day and the humiliation and pain that will follow. Mr. Vigoritti is called to the door; when he returns, his face is ashen. President Kennedy has been shot and killed. Lyndon B. Johnson is the new president.

They all sit stunned. Mr. Vigoritti has told them JFK stories all year. His photo hangs above the blackboard. How could this man be dead?

Later as the boys assemble for the fight, their frustration, anger, and sadness trying to overtake the numbness, Marc steps forward. "I don't care what anybody thinks, we shouldn't be doing this. It's a disgrace! The president is dead somewhere, and we're acting like a bunch of animals." (108) Nicky agrees, and then everyone agrees. It would be a shameful disgrace. Slowly, sadly they drift toward home.

That year, Marc's mom and dad decide to separate. Though Marc hates the new loneliness, the quiet that replaces all the anger and arguing comforts him. He now spends Saturdays with his dad, which helps them develop a better relationship.

The class production of *Julius Caesar* proves a success, Lily and Nicky start going together, Lily's friend Julie catches Marc's attention, and the year ends without the planned fight. Besides losing his first love, Marc has weathered the breakup of his parents and the assassination of President Kennedy. It has been a year to remember.

Activities/Topics for Discussion

- Explain how Nicky fits the stereotype of a bully but Cary does not, although they are both bullies. Compare and contrast these two boys and their bullying behaviors.
- Nicky was a tough kid placed in Mr. Vigoritti's "smart" class. How do you think he felt in this situation? What helped him to be part of the class?
- Using what you know by the end of the book, write a letter to Nicky from Marc about that year.
- Use a crystal ball to predict the future for Marc, Lily, Cary, and Nicky.

- On page 45, Marc has this thought: "People still struggle for power. Small-minded men still murder great ones . . . there are still idealists like Brutus and cynical manipulators like Cassius." Define "idealist" and "cynical manipulators." Who in the book fits "idealist"? Who fits "cynical manipulators"?
- After Nicky got transferred into Mr. Vigoritti's class and got the lead in the play, how do you think his old friends in 6-309 felt?
- This school year was a year of change for many of the students in 6-321. Who do you think changed the most? How did that character change from the beginning of the book to the end?

Quotes for Reader Response

- Nicky Raffetto, the school delinquent, was showing off how his friends could bang into his shoulder but couldn't knock him over. (7)
- He [Cary Lipshitz] was the leader of the cool, tall boys, but a pretty nasty and sarcastic person. (8)
- The bigger, heavier boys in Nicky's class had always hated the smart little skinny guys in my class, . . . Two or three of them used to wait behind a bush now and then to attack one of us, just for fun. (12)
- Here he [Nicky] was, a guy with his own gang of followers, stuck in the middle of thirty-one people who thought to themselves, This boy is *dumb*, every time he opened his mouth. (17)
- Cary went, but his above-it-all grin never changed. That was why the cool boys followed him—because teachers didn't scare him. His parents must have raised him to believe he was better than everyone else, like a prince forced to live among the common folk. (19)
- We ducked behind the thickest, thorniest bushes on the hill, keeping quiet while the creeps yelled, "Come out, you fairies! You can't hide from us!" (32)
- In the past, Cary barely noticed I existed, but now he turned his death-ray eyes on me. Just like I had feared, he used every chance he got to make me look like an idiot. (42)
- Even worse, he started calling me "Spot" because of the mole above my lip. We had a Fall Field Day, and I won the sixty-yard dash . . . but he ruined it by making a wisecrack from the sidelines, "See Spot run." (43)

- Allen brought the rolled-up paintings to school, three guys from Nicky's old class beat him up and tore the paper to shreds. They said they would bash his head in with a brick if he told who did it. (58)
- That must be how feuds work: no matter how wise you think you are, once some bully turns you into a victim, your anger gets the upper hand over your brains. (62)

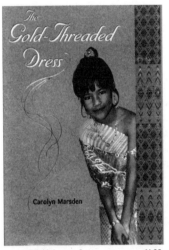

Carolyn Marsden, *The Gold-Threaded Dress.*

Oy and her family moved to the United States because her father got a job as a chef in a Thai restaurant. Here he could make more money, enough to send some back to his mother in Thailand. At home, Oy lives with her parents and her little sister, Luk. They speak Thai and stay close to their Thai heritage. Oy takes lessons in traditional Thai dancing and writes letters in Thai to her grandmother in Bangkok.

Children from many different cultures are in Oy's fourth-grade class. Rohnan's family is from Somalia, Hejski is from Finland, and many students have ancestors from Mexico. Valente, a Native American, is the only one without family roots in another country. The teacher uses a globe to show all these homelands, but Frankie still says Oy is Chinese!

Oy wants to belong to Liliandra's recess club, but Liliandra only chooses those she can benefit from. One day at school, the girls see a photo of Oy in her gold-threaded dress, the one that she wears in her Thai dancing. Liliandra thinks Oy looks like a princess and says if Oy will bring the dress to school for her to try on, Oy may join the club. Oy knows this would be wrong. Her dress is carefully packed away; her grandmother had brought it when she last visited the family. But the temptation to belong to the club is too great, and Oy makes the decision to sneak the dress into school.

During recess Liliandra grabs the dress and marches to her club-house to try it on. Everyone wants to look like a princess and soon they are standing in line to try on the dress. When the recess bell rings, they are rushing, and the dress gets ripped and falls on the ground. The playground aid finds them, in various stages of undress, and takes them to the principal, who blames Oy for bringing the dress and creating such a problem.

Oy's parents are very understanding, realizing that the real problem is that Oy wants friends. Frankie, who is still teasing Oy about being Chinese, becomes her friend and introduces Oy to his Chinese grandfather, Yeh-Yeh. Frankie has been bullied in the past and knows how Oy feels.

Activities/Topics for Discussion

- Frankie teases Oy by pulling his eyes into slits. How does Oy's drawing of her family show he has upset her?
- Children with families from many different countries attend Oy's school. Get a world map and mark all these countries. Are there children in your class with families from other countries? Find these countries on the map. You can do the same thing for students from different states in our country. Talk about these places.
- Why does Oy want to be in Liliandra's club?
- Would you want to be in her club? If you were a member, would you keep other students out of the club? Why?
- The teacher calls Oy "Olivia," giving her an American name. Do you think it is right for the teacher to use a name that is not the student's name?
- Why is Oy upset when Frankie calls her Chinese? Why does he do that?
- Make a chart to show what Oy's life is like at school compared to what her life is like at home.

Quotes for Reader Response

- "Chinese, Japanese." Frankie pulled at the edges of his eyes so that they looked like slits, "Americanese!" (1)
- She glanced up at Frankie's eyes. If only she had eyes like all the others, Frankie wouldn't be teasing her. (4)

- As Oy walked home, she passed the corner of the playground where Liliandra held secret meetings at recess. A girl had to act cool to be invited to join the club. (6)
- "I want Kun Ya [Oy's grandmother] to know that I'm still Thai." (18)
- Oy looked away. She didn't want to seem disappointed. If Liliandra saw that Oy felt let down, she would be even meaner. (23)
- "That dress you were wearing in the picture. You have to bring it to school. You have to let each one of us try it on. . . . Before you get into the clubhouse, you bring the outfit." (23)
- On Sunday mornings, Oy found herself among people who had narrow brown eyes and black hair and silky skin like hers. (32)
- "That dress is too special to bring."
  "Too special?" Liliandra pretended to be surprised. "Nothing is too special for me." (37)
- Maybe it didn't really matter so much if she sacrificed something precious from Thailand in order to have friends at school. (45)
- It would be easy to write a response that looked like Kun Pa's small, neat American writing: "We are very sorry for our daughter's bad actions." Faking his signature would be easy too. (59)
- "A girl wanted to try on the dress. She said she wouldn't be my friend if I didn't bring it to school." (62)
- Oy thought of the way Liliandra teased and demanded. "No, she isn't nice. She's taken all the girls for her friends. I just want to fit in with them. Oh Mere, . . . you don't know how bad it feels to be left out!" (63)
- "To be alone is hard, Oy. But no friend is better than a cruel one." (65)

Graham McNamee, *Nothing Wrong with a Three-Legged Dog.*

Ten-year-old Keath wants to be a golden retriever when he grows up. Fascinated by dogs, Keath researches each breed he meets and keeps a list of them all. He also builds model airplanes from WWII and helps his friend Lynda at her mom's veterinary practice. Keath,–a.k.a. Whitey, Va-nilla, or Mayonnaise–is so much more than the only white kid in his fourth-grade class at Frederick Douglass Elementary School. Lynda gets called Zebra because her mother is black and her father is white. Everyone at school gets called a name, even Toothpick, who is so skinny his bones stick out and his elbows and knees looks like sharp weapons. Toothpick and his henchman, Blob, make Keath's life miserable.

After school, Keath and Lynda wash and cuddle dogs to help Lynda's mom, and walk dogs and scoop poop to help her dad, a professional dog walker. Keath loves Lynda's dog, Leftovers, a happy and loveable beagle with a great attitude who doesn't let it bother him that he lost an ear and a back leg after a car hit him.

At school Toothpick's bullying intensifies after Keath sees Toothpick's older brother bullying Toothpick. It isn't until Toothpick starts making fun of Leftovers that Keath finds the courage to stand up to the bully.

Activities/Topics for Discussion

- "Like the chameleon, . . . If I could just change colors when I need to. I mean, then there would be no problems.

    No. It's just if you're the right color, you fit in. But the right color keeps changing, so it's better if you can change too." (14) What is Keath talking about? Why would he want to change colors? Is there a right color?

- In the book, there are hints that tell us why Toothpick is a bully. What makes him a bully? Why does Toothpick bully other kids, particularly Keath and Lynda?
- Keath takes the bullying until Toothpick makes fun of Leftovers. Why does that matter to him? Why does Keath stand up for Leftovers when he doesn't stand up for himself? Is there someone that you protect? Is there someone who protects you?
- People get bullied for many different things. Keath and Lynda are picked on because of their race. Why? Make a list of all the racist comments made in the book. Have you ever heard any of these?
- At this school, everyone seems to have a nickname. List all those names and decide if they are positive or negative names. On a separate piece of paper, make a list of all the names you have been called. Which ones are positive and which are negative? How can you respond to the negative names?
- In the beginning of the book, Keath feels like an outsider at school. His father suggests that Keath switch schools, but Keath wants to stay at Frederick Douglass Elementary School, and by the end of the book, he likes it there. What has changed?
- Why was Keath afraid to go see his grandmother? What did he discover when he did go visit her?

Quotes for Reader Response

- Lynda says when they call her Zebra she thinks about the horse with the Mohawk, and the name doesn't hurt so bad. (1)
- I had just gotten out of detention. I was sentenced to two hours' detention for fighting, and I didn't even fight back, just got punched. (5)
- "It's just that if you're the right color, you fit in. But the right color keeps changing, so it's better if you can change too. One day you're brown, one day you're green." (14)
- I don't know why Toothpick and Blob hate me so much. But I know if I looked like everybody else, I wouldn't be their main target. (28)
- "Some kids look at me and say that I'm black, then some say I'm more white than black, or not black enough. It's stupid. Maybe I'm just Lynda, you know?" (80–1)
- "So I get whacked at school because I'm Whitey, and your dad's family won't see you because you're only half white." I do a big shrug. "You can't win." (90)

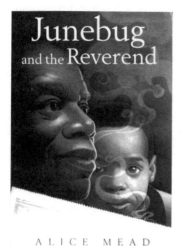

A L I C E   M E A D

Alice Mead, *Junebug and the Reverend.*

Reeve McClain Jr., a.k.a. Junebug, his sister Tasha, and their mom leave the projects when Mrs. McClain gets a job as a residence supervisor for a senior citizens' apartment building. While Tasha, 6, and Reeve, 10, finish the last three weeks of the school year in a new district, Mrs. McClain is busy learning all the details of her new job and getting to know the first two residents, Miss Rosalie Williams and Reverend Ashford.

Miss Williams, a very active and vibrant woman, practices Tai Chi and becomes good friends with Tasha. Reverend Ashford, cranky and resentful about having to move there, has damaged lungs and keeps oxygen in his apartment. Every morning, Junebug and the Reverend go for a walk to get a newspaper and Reverend Ashford sneaks a cigarette. Walter, the Reverend's son, helps handle his father and shows a growing interest in Junebug's mom.

At school, Junebug sees Greg and a few of his buddies put tacks on Brandon's seat. Brandon, a timid, small boy, makes an easy target, and after he sits on the tacks, he puts his head down and cries. Junebug shows his disgust of the bullies and after school they jump him. Because his mom worries about his having new friends at school, Junebug makes Tasha promise not to tell. However, he has begun to start confiding in Reverend Ashford, and the two grow closer.

But there is too much for Junebug to deal with: a new home, missing his best friend Robert and his old neighborhood, the bullies at school, and accepting the fact that his father, who is in prison, has never tried to contact him. Plus Junebug's mom, who always used to have time for him, has a new job and a new relationship with Walter. Junebug is not happy.

As the school year comes to an end, Mrs. McClain decides Junebug should sign up to play in the summer soccer league. The practices are demanding, but the real complication is Greg and his friends, who are there bossing Junebug and Brandon. Reverend Ashford and

Tasha attend their first game. It is an exciting game until Greg pulls some of his bullying stunts. Coach Olson sees it and forfeits the game. As the coach is talking to the team, Tasha comes running up. Reverend Ashford is having trouble breathing. Junebug runs to him and applies all of the emergency techniques his mother taught him. Soon the EMTs arrive and take over. The Reverend will be okay, but there will not be any more morning cigarettes.

In the few weeks since they have moved in, Junebug has matured. Mr. Olson, his teacher and coach, told Junebug he had leadership abilities. Without realizing it, Junebug had put those abilities into action by supporting Brandon and helping Reverend Ashford, and he has gained more confidence. When the Reverend gets home, Junebug and Walter are going to plant a tree by the bench where Reverend Ashford can sit and read the newspaper in the fresh morning air.

Activities/Topics for Discussion

- How did Junebug get his name? How does his need to ask questions help him? Hurt him?
- Have you ever been the "new kid"? What was it like?
- In the beginning of the book, Junebug has some strong thoughts about old people. What are those thoughts? Do they change by the end of the book?
- Make a list of all the ways Greg bullies other students.
- Why is Brandon an easy target?
- Use a graphic organizer to show what Brandon is like in the beginning of the book and what he is like by the end.
- What does Brandon do to thank Junebug for helping him against the bullies and to prove he wants to be Junebug's friend?
- Compare and contrast Junebug and Greg. Use a graphic organizer to visualize your thoughts.
- Sometimes secrets need to be told. How do we know when it is necessary to tell a secret?

Quotes for Reader Response

- Brandon's so puny that it doesn't seem fair for anybody to pick on him. What's the point! I give them a frowny look that says, Grow up! (39)

- Mr. Olson says recess is the most important part of our day. That's when we learn to treat each other with respect. He demands it. And he gets it most of the time because he plays fair. (44)
- I don't think kids should pick on weaklings like Brandon, but if I go eat lunch with him . . . he'll probably turn into a great big Mr. Tag-a-long and follow me around for the rest of my entire life, and that would mean nobody else in the school would ever be friends with me. (45)
- I guess kids can become bullies even when they have fancy new overalls and moms who pick them up in minivans. (45)
- Greg says, "Listen, trash lover, you tell on us and you're dead." (53)
- "My teacher tells our class, if big kids come up to you on the playground, go get help. So I did." (59)
- "The world needs kids with leadership qualities." (83)
- "I think about Brandon in his little apartment over the garage and how he's not really white. He's more sort of faded into no color at all." (137)
- "I'm sorry that we ganged up on you at school and that Greg tripped you today."

    "Yeah? When your friend acts like a jerk and fights dirty, you need to tell him where to get off. How come you let that kid run your life?"

    "I don't know." (156)
- "When people keep secrets from each other in a family, it can hurt worse than lying. Usually we keep secrets about things we're ashamed of." (160–61)

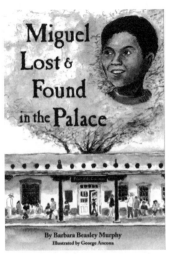

By Barbara Beasley Murphy
Illustrated by George Ancona

Barbara Beasley Murphy
Miguel Lost & Found in the Palace.
George Anacona, Illlustrator.

Often harassment is about being different. Usually that difference is not a bad thing, but if a bully objects to it for any reason, he or she can make the other person feel self-conscious. In this book, several people bully Miguel because he and his family are Mexican. That is how they are different; that is what threatens the bullies. Sometimes adults behave as poorly as the children when faced with things unfamiliar to them.

In the middle of the night, five-year-old Miguel sits on the shoulders of his father, Crístobel Rivera, as they and Miguel's mother, Rosa, cross the Rio Grande and illegally enter the United States. Three years later, the family now lives in El Paso, Texas and includes three-years-old-twins, Oprah and Carla, and eight-year-old Maria Contenta. Miguel is in Mr. Springley's wonderful third-grade class. Joey Jeter Cortés, another student in Mr. Springley's class, is prejudiced against Mexicans and regularly beats up on Miguel. Outside of Mr. Springley's influence, things are not good at school, and though Miguel has a loving family, tension increases at home.

When his father goes to his night watchman job, men come and try to convince him to help them smuggle people across the border. When Crístobel refuses, they beat him. When Rosa finds out, she decides her husband must leave for Albuquerque immediately, as someone there has promised them work. A few days later, the Immigration and Naturalization Service (INS) visits their home looking for Crístobel. Rosa tells them nothing, and because Crístobel has not contacted her, she honestly does not know where he is. Rosa packs up the kids, and they all go to Albuquerque, where they discover Crístobel never arrived. Rosa cannot go to the authorities, so they have no way to search for him.

School in Albuquerque has the same prejudiced bullies as El Paso, though Miguel does find Albert King for a friend. When the family moves to Santa Fe for Rosa's job, the same attitude against Mexicans seems to exist there. However, Albert King has friends in Santa Fe, and he asks them to contact Miguel. These friends teach Miguel about Mexico's role in New Mexico's history. While the Rivera family tries to cope without their father in yet another new city, Crístobel is held prisoner by smugglers who pack immigrants in the back of trucks and sneak them across the border. He manages to free himself and agrees to help the INS prosecute the smugglers. The family receives word of his release, and the next day, when Miguel leaves school, he is greeted by Crístobel.

Activities/Topics for Discussion

- Miguel is called several ethnic hate slurs in the book. Make a list of them and try to explain their meaning. Why are these words hurtful?
- Make a list of other hate slurs you have heard. Why are they powerful and hurtful put-downs?
- We all are judged by what we say. Every word that comes out of our mouths labels us in one way or another. How is Miguel judged by his speech? How is Joey judged by his words?
- In each town where Miguel lives, he has one good friend. List these friends. What common qualities do they have? How do their friendships help Miguel?
- The readers know that Joey's father, Sergeant Richard Cortés, an INS officer, entered the country illegally. Why do you think he keeps that a secret? Do you think people harassed him when he was in school the same way his son harasses Miguel? Explain.
- How does knowing Santa Fe's history help Miguel feel less threatened?
- Have you ever been the "new kid" at school, in a class, a neighborhood? If you have, what did it feel like to come to a new place where everyone knows everyone else, but you don't know anyone?
- Do you know anyone who was born in another country? If you do, interview that person about how people accepted him/her in their new country.
- How could you be a kind friend to a new student from another school? From another country?

Quotes for Reader Response

- "Snot nose!" Joey Jeter Cortés hissed, leaning over, and punching Miguel's shoulder another two times. "You act so smart. You show off! You're dumb." (19)
- The kid knocking him around in the classroom also used him for punching at recess. (20)
- "I don't have new clothes, . . . I don't look good to kids. So they hit me. I need a baseball cap. To be cool. Like the other kids. Not so poor." (21)
- "Chicanos! Mojados. Wetbacks!" the bigger boys yelled, making faces. "Go home. Back to Mexico! We don't want you here. You stink." (30)
- "Miguel, tell 'em what your mom got you." Albert said.
  "Oh! A bike, so I can get away from the kids who hate me." (74)
- Miguel was shocked to learn that the Indians here [Santa Fe] were admired. How different from Mexico! He knew that the Indians there were often looked down upon and nobody wanted to be them. (87)
- Sitting on the bench now, he felt the cold loneliness of being new to Santa Fe and the Ortiz Middle School. . . . Sooner or later Miguel knew he was going to be picked on and even kicked around. (88)
- No matter what, his spirit was created stonger than the cruelty of mean boys. (98)
- "No matter how they mess you up in school—not the teachers, I mean, the doofy kids—you're going to get smart! It's the only thing that makes 'em respect you, Miguel" (108)
- I'm going to find out something here that I can do with my whole life. Maybe be a photographer and take pictures of all the different kinds of kids in the world to show people. (121–2)
- "If we talk about prejudice honestly, we can deal with it and make things better." (129)

Kathleen O'Dell, *Agnes Parker . . . Girl in Progress.*

Agnes Parker is keeping her fingers crossed that she and her best friend, Prejean Duval, will be in the same sixth-grade class this year. That way Prejean will be there to protect Agnes from Neidermeyer—"one of the last girls who still loves to sock people." (10) Peggy Neidermeyer also loves to torment "Gagness." From name-calling to dodge ball bombs thrown from third-floor apartments, she has it in for Agnes.

On the first day of school, Agnes and Prejean find out that they are both in Mrs. Libonati's class, but so is Neidermeyer. Joe Waldrip, a new student, also joins the class. Mrs. Libonati is a no-nonsense type of teacher, and on the first day, she assigns their first report. Each student will research a Native American. Agnes gets Squanto, and the class breaks into laughter led by Neidermeyer. Exiled to the hallway, Neidermeyer signals Agnes that the war is on!

Joe and his father and little brother have moved in with Joe's grandmother, who happens to live next door to Agnes. They get to know each other over the backyard fence and become friends while working on their Native American reports. Joe confides in Agnes that his mom has recently died. His father quit his job and moved the family in with Joe's grandmother so she could help. Joe's dad misses his wife terribly and seems to be sinking into a depression. Agnes promises to keep Joe's secrets private.

Peggy Neidermeyer also befriends Joe. They are both athletes and have a lot in common. Though Agnes isn't threatened by their friendship, Neidermeyer does not like Agnes' friendship with Joe, and that fuels the harassment. Prejean feels burdened by her need to take care of Agnes and tells her that, so Agnes tries to be braver.

Agnes is a person in progress, a nice person with morals, a conscience, and a kind heart. She looks at her behavior and tries to do what is right. Prejean and Joe are both her friends, but she doesn't understand how she and Peggy can both be Joe's friends, as Peggy doesn't really deserve friends. Joe just shrugs and says, "You two are just different." When Joe's father decides that the family needs to go back to their hometown, Peggy breaks down in class when she hears the news. Agnes understands because she feels sad, too.

Activities/Topics for Discussion

- Make a chart. On one side list all the bullying behaviors children do in grades 1–3, and on the other side list all the behaviors children do in the intermediate grades. Why did the behaviors change? Maybe all these behaviors should stop. What do you think?
- Agnes secretly writes a note to the teacher explaining how Pat Marie gets teased. What are some things that you could do to help someone who is being bullied?
- Prejean and Agnes have an argument, and as Prejean walks away, Agnes reaches out and snaps her bra strap. There are other kids around and they start teasing her. Is that bullying? What would be a good definition of bullying?
- After Agnes gives her speech as Squanto, she goes back to her seat and has trouble concentrating. "She is mesmerized by what she did, what she said." (84) What emotion do you think she is feeling? Tell a time when you felt that proud of yourself.
- In the book, Peggy Neidermeyer is almost always called by her last name. What affect does that create? How does it add to her image?
- Use a graphic organizer to show what Agnes thought of Neidermeyer at the beginning of the book and what she thought of her by the end.

Quotes for Reader Response

- *Ka-thwap*! Agnes feels a rubbery smack against her head accompanied by a deep echoing bong! She wobbles and almost falls off her bike. . . . *Ow, ow, ow . . . Neidermeyer!* (10)
- Neidermeyer has obviously trained her sights on Agnes. When she passes, she squinches up her eye and sneers.
  "Yo, Professor Geek. . . . How's them four eyes?" (29)
- "Just some mean kids at school." she [Agnes] says.
  "Are they hitting people?" asks Mr. Parker.
  "Oh, you know. They call people fat or gay and make fun of them. . . ."
  "Some things never change," says Mr. Parker. (40)

- "It is not everyone who can take another person's feeling as seriously as they do their own. That is the ingredient needed to be a good friend—and a good person." (48)
- "I will fight no more forever." (58)
- "You can't just let everyone pick on you like this." says Prejean.
  "I'm not letting people pick on me."
  "Well, yes, you sort of are." (78)
- "Squanto!" Agnes feels the hot word in her ear. She turns to see Neidermeyer and Carmella, who salute her with a quick sticking-out of their tongues before pushing past her. (81)
- "Why don't you and Hagness Puker just hang out in dorkville for the rest of the night?" (98)
- "Usually," she explains, "people sort of take sides. But you're nice to practically everybody." (125)
- "You are a great friend to have, Agnes Parker. And you should know that about yourself." (151)

ADDY
LEARNS
A LESSON
A SCHOOL STORY
~ BOOK TWO ~

Connie Porter, *Addy Learns a Lesson: A School Story*, *The American Girls Collection*, Book Two. Melodye Rosales, Illustrator.

The year is 1864, and Addy Walker and her mother have come north from North Carolina. After Addy's father and brother, Sam, were sold off the plantation, Addy and her mother left baby sister Ester with Auntie Lula and Uncle Solomon before they ran away from Master Steven's plantation. As they stand on the pier in Philadelphia, a new life of freedom awaits them. Mrs. Moore and her daughter, Sarah, from the Freedom Society arrive and take them to the church for a meal and a sense of community. Sarah and her family had been slaves in Virginia. Mrs. Moore helps Mrs. Walker find a sewing job and a place for them to stay.

For the first time, Addy is able to attend school and is very anxious to learn how to read and write. Sarah helps Addy at school and teaches her other things, like how to read street signs and addresses and how to get around the city. Mrs. Dunn, their teacher, gives Addy a new desk partner, Harriet Davis, a very smart girl with lots of attitude. Harriet has always been a free person and seems to think that makes her better than those who have been slaves. Addy thinks Harriet's dresses are beautiful and wants to be her friend. Sarah warns Addy to be careful because last year Harriet had been unkind to her.

One day Harriet asks Addy to walk home with her and her friends. Addy wants Sarah to walk with them, but she won't. When Addy catches up with Harriet and the others, they give Addy all of their books to carry. Harrirt says Addy can be their "flunky." After a few days of this abuse, Addy realizes Harriet is treating her like a slave—and Addy is letting her. After Addy beats Harriet in a spelling match, Harriet shuns her.

The story continues in book 3, *Addy's Surprise: A Christmas Story* in this American Girls Collection.

Activities/Topics for Discussion

- Cite examples of how Sarah is a good friend to Addy from the first day they met.
- Sarah and Addy can't ride on the streetcars because they are "colored." This is an example of racism. How are racism and bullying alike? How are they different?
- Use a graphic organizer to compare and contrast Sarah and Harriet.
- Why is Addy so fascinated by Harriet?
- Why do Harriet and her other friends bully Addy and Sarah?
- What is a "flunky?"
- During the spelling match, Sarah spells a word wrong and is eliminated. Addy is next and has to spell the same word. Though Addy knows how to spell the word correctly, she considers spelling it wrong on purpose. Why would she do that? What makes her spell it correctly? What would you do?
- Miss Dunn thinks Addy has learned a lesson about friendship. What do you think Addy has learned?

Quotes for Reader Response

- "Addy, Harriet don't like me. She all stuck-up. She think she better than other people. If your family ain't got no money, she don't like you. And you know my family poor." (28)
- "Harriet don't have no poor girls like us for her friends. She gonna try to make you her slave." (29)
- But Addy liked to think about Harriet. Harriet had everything that Addy dreamed freedom would bring *her*. (36)
- Harriet turned around in her seat and said to Sarah, "You know the war is going to free the slaves. You should be glad for the war. *You* were a slave yourself." (42)
- "Not me. My family has always been free." Harriet said proudly. (42)
- "We don't need to do or say anything that draws more lines between people. The entire country has been divided in two. Let's not make differences based on who was a slave or wasn't, or *anything* else." (42)
- Harriet handed Addy her books. One by one, the other girls piled their books on top.

   "These are kinda heavy," Addy said. "Why I got to carry them all?"

   "Well, if you want to be with us, you have to be our flunky," Harriet said. (46)
- "Did you see Sarah today?" Harriet said in a mean voice. "Her dress was so wrinkled, it looked like she slept in it." (51)
- "Her [Sarah's] mother is a washerwoman, and she can't even keep Sarah's clothes clean," said Harriet.

   All the girls laughed, except for Addy. (52)
- "Addy looks good enough to be our flunky, though," Mavis said. (53)
- Harriet did not want Addy to be her friend. She just wanted Addy to be her slave. And even worse, Addy had *chosen* to be her slave. (54)

Trevor Romain, *Bullies Are a Pain in the Brain.* Nonfiction.

If I could give only one book to every student, teacher, administrator, staff member, and parent, it would be this nonfiction book. The language makes it accessible to even the youngest child, the practical advice makes it valuable to adults, and the cartoon-like illustrations make it attractive to kids of all ages.

Romain starts by defining what bullies are and what they do. Bullies like to control. That's how they feel superior. If the bully isn't bullying, she/he feels inferior. Although bullies are good at bullying people, they are not good at making friends. They do not know how to be kind, helpful, share, or talk nicely with others. Instead they give mean looks, embarrass, shove, tease, threaten, harass, and hurt others' feelings.

The book coaches kids how to react to a bully's harassment. Crying is definitely not a good response; neither is blaming oneself, keeping it a secret, or feeling ashamed. Romain calls bullies self-esteem vampires, as they can suck the self-confidence right out of you. So victims should tell someone if they are being bullied. Such secrets keep us worried, frightened, ashamed. The target didn't do anything wrong; telling someone shares the problem and that makes it smaller.

Romain also lists the top-five myths about bullying:

- Bullies have low self-esteem, which is why they pick on other people.
- Only boys are bullies.
- Getting bullied is a normal part of growing up.
- The best way to handle a bully is by getting even or fighting back.
- If you ignore them, bullies will go away. (46–50)

As adults we have heard these statements so often and for so long that accepting they are false may take some work. For all of us—parents, teachers, administrators—there is much to learn about the issues of bullying and harassment.

Romain suggests several solutions: One is for the students to ask teachers to hold a bully workshop. Most of us couldn't do that without some footwork. But there may be someone on the staff who could present a workshop, and the first trained should be the staff. Before we teach anything to our students, we have to educate ourselves.

This book includes a twelve-question quiz, "Are You a Bully?" As these particular school years are a crucial time to work with those who bully, this quiz and Romain's suggestions for reforming the bully are needed ingredients to any anti-bullying program. Bullies need help before they get locked into these harmful behaviors.

Activities/Topics for Discussion

There are several good activities in *Bullies Are a Pain in the Brain*. Here are some others I have used:

* With the class's help, create a bully map/graphic organizer on the board. Write the word "bully" in a circle. Ask the students to name bullying behaviors. Place each example in a circle and connect that circle to the Bully Circle. When the kids have trouble finding examples, expand on the different names used as put-downs, or list the places in the building where bullying most likely happens. Not only does this give the students a chance to speak up, but it also provides needed information for the staff.
* Make a list of things students could do if they saw someone being bullied.
* Ask if any of their favorite TV shows have bullies in them. Discuss how the bully behaves, how the target feels, how the bully feels, and what makes the bully behave this way.
* Tell about a time when you were a bully. (I confess stories from when I had to baby-sit my three younger sisters and resorted to bullying.)
* Use the children's story, "The Three Little Pigs." Role play the three little pigs handling the Big Bad Wolf. Ask someone to role play the Big Bad Wolf and tell his side. How could the three little pigs and the Big Bad Wolf help each other and get to be friends? I have had high school sophomores write new scripts covering some of these scenes.

- Make a list of other children's stories that contain bullies. Do some more role-playing.

Quotes for Reader Response

- Experts tell us that bullies like to be in control. By controlling you, a bully feels strong and superior. And you feel puny, afraid—and angry. (3)
- There's one thing bullies have in common: they like to be in charge. The more they drain the self-esteem of others, the better they feel. (7)
- Bullies harm people in many different ways—physicially, mentally, and emotionally. (10)
- Bullies think they've hit the jackpot when they make you cry. (23)
- Don't let a bully take away your self-esteem. Find your strengths and achieve your goals. (39)
- Believe it or not, people can actually bully *themselves*. (40)
- Friends are for sticking by you in tough times. Tell your friends if you're being bullied. (44)
- Because it isn't easy to communicate with a bully, you might want to rehearse what you'll say. (53)
- Don't be afraid to tell an adult if you're being bullied. . . . You are NOT a tattletale if you report someone who's hurting you. (57)
- By reporting a bully, you're helping yourself and others. Think of all the other kids the bully picks on each day. (58)
- Taunting a bully is like teasing a vicious dog. (65)
- If you get in a fight, you have nothing to gain and everything to lose. (71)
- Want to surprise a bully? Try making friends with him! (81)

Jerry Spinelli, *Maniac Magee.*

Jeffrey Lionel Magee became an orphan at age three and was moved to the divided house of his Aunt Dot and Uncle Dan. For eight years he lived with two people who never shared anything—not a meal, not a hobby, not a word, not even space. Jeffrey couldn't take the hostility and the silence, and he started running, observing, and saying "hi" to everyone he passed. Slowly everyone starts to notice the scrawny little white boy who can run while reading a book, hit John McNab's fast-ball pitches when no one else could touch them, race through a football game and score a touchdown, and run on the steel rails of a train track—right on the rails! This kid is incredible, this kid can do everything, this kid will risk anything, he is a maniac of legendary proportion—Maniac Magee.

In Two Mills, there is the West End and the East End, but Maniac doesn't know that. He runs everywhere, talks to everyone, sleeps wherever he can—sometimes in the deer shed at the zoo, sometimes in the East End and sometimes in the West End. Maniac doesn't realize West End and East End are two separate worlds. Only blacks live in East End and only whites live in West End—another divided world. Only Maniac manages to live in both. When Mrs. Beale finds out Maniac slept in the zoo's deer shed, she invites him to join the family. Hester and Lester, the youngest Beales are terrors until Maniac tames them; now, they take baths together every night. "One little black girl, one little black boy, one medium white boy. And she [Mrs. Beale] would smile and wag her head and sigh: 'Never saw such a tub'." (48)

Maniac is happy, he has a family and an address, but then someone decided "Whitey" did not belong, and could not possibly fit in to East End. But then somebody writes "Fishbelly Go Home" on the Beale's house, Maniac leaves to protect the family. Again Maniac doesn't have a home. He returns to the zoo, this time sleeping in the buffalo pen where Earl Grayson, a zoo worker, discovers him. As only Maniac can make happen, the old man and the boy bond and become family. Grayson, a former minor-league baseball pitcher, teaches him about baseball, and Maniac teaches Grayson how to read. They share a wonderful daily life, and then one morning, when Maniac tries to wake Grayson, the old man is dead. Maniac is an orphan again. Maniac disappears.

Russell and Piper McNab run away every few weeks, and this time the two little brothers hide out in a tiny cabin in Valley Forge and find Maniac. They take Maniac home where he meets their older brother, John McNab, the little league pitcher whose strikeout record Maniac ended. For a while, Maniac moves in with John's red-necked, phobic, bigoted family that is made up of only males: father, three sons, and various cousins. While he is living there, Maniac also reconnects with one of his first bullies from East End, Mars Bar Thompson, writer of "Fishbelly Go Home." Again Magee sees how hate can divide people, but life has taught him how to deal with it. They don't all hug and bond as a family, but each learns a bit about the humanness of the other. By the end of the book, Mars Bar, renamed Snickers, has become one of Jeffrey Lionel Magee's guardian angels.

Activities/Topics for Discussion

- What in Maniac's life has kept him from being prejudiced? Why doesn't he see a difference between white skin and black skin?
- On pages 91 and 92, when Grayson explains his baseball past, he says he was a pitcher with such proud declaration that Maniac could tell Grayson was more than he appeared. How are you more than what you show in your classroom? Make a list of things about you that most people in the class do not know. What on that list are you most proud of?
- Have you ever met someone and didn't like him/her for some reason, and then when you got to know that person, that reason didn't seem so important? Share the experience with the class. What happened?
- Maniac gets picked on for many things. Make a list of all the things people use to make fun of Maniac. Why doesn't he let that bother him?
- Why wouldn't Maniac spend the night at Mars Bar's house?
- How might Maniac define the word, "home"?
- How does Maniac seem to change people?

Quotes for Reader Response

- Some say he [Maniac] only intended to pause here but that he stayed because he was so happy to make a friend. (8)
- Arnold Jones was being hoisted in the air above Finsterwald's backyard fence. The hoisters were three or four high school kids. This was one of the things they did for fun. (17)
- Hecter Street was the boundary between the East and West Ends. Or, to put it another way, between the blacks and whites. (32)
- Maniac felt a hard flatness against his back. Suddenly his world was very small and very simple: a brick wall behind him, a row of scowling faces in front of him. (39)
- Maniac loved the colors of the East End. The people colors. (51)
- Inside his house, a kid gets one name, but on the other side of the door, it's whatever the rest of the world wants to call him. (53)
- He couldn't see that Mars Bar disliked him, maybe even hated him. (57)
- "You move on now, Whitey," the man said. "You pick up your gear and move on out." (60)
- FISHBELLY GO HOME (63)
- The hatred in Mars Bar's eyes was no longer for a white kid in the East End; it was for Jeffrey Magee, period. (148)
- The East Enders stayed in the east and the West Enders stayed in the west, and the less they knew about each other, the more they invented. (159)
- He was quite content to let Amanda do the talking, for he knew that behind her grumbling was all that he had ever wanted. He knew that finally, truly, at long last, someone was calling him home. (184)

Annotated Bibliography

Some books are also appropriate for other levels. P-Primary, M-Middle School.

Ayres, Katherine. *Macaroni Boy*. New York: Delacorte Press, 2003. Mike Costa lives in Pittsburgh with his Italian-Irish family during the 1930s depression. He also has a running battle with Andy Simms, who constantly harasses Mike at school. When Mike's grandpap gets sick and Andy shows the same symptoms, Mike decides it is time to make peace with Andy.

Bates, Betsy. Illustrated by Leslie Morrill. *Tough Beans*. New York: Holiday House, 1988. Nat Berger has diabetes, and suddenly he has to learn new rules—what to eat, how to give himself shots, and how to deal with Jasper Denletter, the new bully in town.

Calhoun, B. B. Illustrated by Daniel Mark Duffy. *Fair Play*. New York: W. H. Freeman and Company, 1994. Fenton Rumplemayer helps his dad and his team of paleontologists uncover dinosaur fossils at a dig site in Wyoming. This year Fen's sixth-grade class is having a Dinosaur Science Fair. Everything seems to fit together until Buster, the class bully, resents the attention Fenton keeps getting. This book contains terrific facts about dinosaurs.

Clements, Andrew. *The Jacket*. New York: Simon & Schuster, 2002. Phil Morelli, a white sixth grader has to find his younger brother to give him lunch money. Phil spots his brother's jacket but after he reaches out to grab his arm, a black kid turns around. What goes through Phil's mind then and after makes him wonder if he is prejudiced—is he one of the privileged white kids who picks on others?

Coville, Bruce. *The Monster's Ring*. New York: Harcourt, 1982, 2002. Fifth grader Russell Crannaker gets bullied at school and at home. Everything changes when he stumbles into Mr. Elives magic shop and buys a Monster's Ring. Now he can turn himself into a monster with just a twist of the ring, but Russell soon realizes how exciting and dangerous this power can be.

Crisp, Marty. Illustrated by True Kelly. *My Dog, Cat*. New York: Holiday House, 2000. Abbott Williamson III, known as Abbie, wants a big dog named Killer to protect him from Pete Street, the fourth-grade bully. But what Abbie gets is his aunt's Yorkshire terrier named Cat while she vacations. Cat has enough attitude to take on the world—and Pete Street.

Davis, Gibb. Illustrated by Abby Carter. *Camp Sink or Swim*. New York: Random House, 1997. Because Danny is almost nine years old, his parents have decided to let him go to Camp Kickapoo for the summer with his best friend Billy. Even though Danny is excited, he realizes that the other kids, particularly the bully Tonya, will find out that his stories about being a champion swimmer are lies. A liar and a bully learn a lot about friendship. (P)

Deans, Sis. *Racing the Past*. New York: Henry Holt, 2001. After his violent father dies, eleven year-old Ricky gets into fights when bullies taunt him. He makes a deal with the principal: to avoid the bullies he will never share the same space with them, which means no recess or school bus. He walks, and then runs, to and from school.

De Guzman, Michael. *Melonhead*. New York: Farrar, Straus & Giroux, 2002. Sidney, a short, slim, twelve-year-old, has a head as big as a cantaloupe and his last name is Melon! His mother and stepfather live in Seattle, his father lives in Los Angeles, and Sidney is sick of being shuffled back and forth, so he buys a bus ticket and starts across the country.

Gorman, Carol. *Dork in Disguise*. New York: HarperCollins, 1999. A dork in his old school, Jerry Flack has spent the whole summer re-searching how to be cool so he fits in better at his new middle school.

Hiser, Constance. Illustrated by Cat Bowman Smith. *Ghosts in Fourth Grade*. New York: Holiday House, 1991. James and his friends have a plan to get revenge on Mean Mitchell, the school bully. On Halloween they take over the old haunted Hathaway House and play lots of tricks on Mean Mitchell.

Holt, Kimberly Willis. *When Zachary Beaver Came to Town*. New York: Holt, 1999. Toby Wilson thinks nothing exciting ever hap-pens in Antler, Texas, until his mother wins a chance to sing at the Grand Ole Opry, his best friend's brother writes home from Viet Nam, and Zachary Beaver, the fattest boy in the world, comes to town. (M)

Laser, Michael. *6-321*. New York: Atheneum, 2001. Set in Queens during the sixties, Marc Chaikin faces the challenges of sixth grade, bullies, falling in love, and accepting some hard realities. (M)

Marsden, Carolyn. *The Gold-Threaded Dress*. Cambridge, MA: Can-dlewick Press, 2002. Although Oy is from Thailand, the students in her fourth-grade class call her Chinita, Spanish for little Chinese. What she wants most is to be accepted by Lilianda and invited to her club house, and if Oy brings her traditional Thai dress to school that might happen.

McKenzie, Ellen Kindt. *Under the Bridge*. New York: Henry Holt, 1994. Ritchie is ten years old and carrying the weight of the world on his shoulders. His mother is in the hospital, his little sister is very sick, his father rarely communicates, and a school bully tor-tures him.

McNamee, Graham. *Nothing Wrong with a Three-Legged Dog.* New York: Random House, 2000. Keath gets called Whitey because he is the only white kid in his fourth-grade class. He and his best friend Lynda, who is biracial, find the courage to stand up to the bullies when they have to protect Lynda's three-legged beagle. (P)

Meacham, Margartet. *Quiet! You're Invisible.* New York: Holiday House, 2001. Hoby Hobson, fifth grader, has enough problems due to the seventh grade bully, Harold "Hammerhead" Jones, and then Zirc Orflandu flies into Hoby's backyard—from the future. While Hoby and Zirc try to fix Zirc's space cruiser and keep Zirc hidden, Hammerhead steals the cruiser's battery.

Mead, Alice. *Junebug and the Reverend.* New York: Random House, 1998. Junebug and his family move out of the projects when his mother gets a new job as Resident Supervisor of a senior citizen apartment building. Besides all that, Junebug has to adjust to a new school and new bullies. (P)

Millman, Dan. Illustrated by T. Taylor Bruce. *Secret of the Peaceful Warrior.* Tiburon, CA: H. J. Krammer, 1991. On the first day at his new school, Danny Morgan attracts the attention of Carl, the school bully. With the help of Socrates, a friend's grandfather, Danny learns the lessons of a peaceful warrior. (P)

Murphy, Barbara Beasley. *Miguel Lost & Found in the Palace.* Santa Fe, NM: Museum of New Mexico Press, 2002. Miguel and his parents cross the Rio Grande into Texas to start a new life, but this new country brings many hardships, including the prejudice Miguel faces at school.

Myers, Laurie. Illustrated by Dan Yaccarino. *Surviving Brick Johnson.* New York: Clarion Books, 2000. Fifth-grader Alex makes fun of Brick Johnson, not realizing that Brick is watching. Although Alex's younger brother says Brick would not hurt him, Alex spends most of the book trying to survive his blunder.

O'Dell, Kathleen. *Agnes Parker . . . Girl in Progress.* New York: Dial Books, 2003. Sixth grade brings new challenges for Agnes, who has to learn independence and strength to deal with the class bully, Peggy Neidermeyer.

Park, Barbara. *Dear God, Help—Love Earl.* New York: Knopf, 1993. Earl Wilbur, an overweight boy with asthma, is bullied by Eddy McFee. Earl thinks that he has the problem solved when he starts paying Eddy to leave him alone.

Porter, Connie. Illustrated by Melodye Rosales. *Addy Learns a Lesson: A School Story.* The American Girls Collection, Book Two. New

York: Scholastic, 1994. Addy and her mother are escaped slaves
when they reach Philadelphia. Addy goes to school to learn to read
and write and discovers some unexpected prejudices.

Roberts, Willo Davis. *The Kidnappers*. New York: Atheneum, 1998.
Eleven-year-old Joey has a problem with a bully at school. Then he
sees the bully kidnapped, but no one will believe him.

Romain, Trevor. *Bullies Are a Pain in the Brain*. Minneapolis, MN:
Free Spirit, 1997. Nonfiction. This book about bullies and how to
handle them is done with clarity, illustrations, and humor. Besides
being informative, it presents defense strategies and advice for students, school staff, and parents. (P, M)

———. *Cliques, Phonies, & Other Baloney*. Minneapolis, MN: Free
Spirit Publishing, 1998. Nonfiction. With the same format as *Bullies Are a Pain in the Brain*, this book suggests ways to avoid the
cliques and create meaningful, healthy friendships. (M)

Sathre, Vivian. Illustrated by Catharine O'Neill. *J. B. Wigglebottom
and the Parade of Pets*. New York: Atheneum, 1993. J. B. gets
bullied by Buddy Zimms, but he also bullies his younger sister,
Kate, his biggest fan. Because of Kate's allergies, J. B. doesn't
have a pet to enter in the Parade of Pets, unless he can think of a
really clever plan, and he does.

Scrimger, Richard. *The Nose from Jupiter*. Toronto: Tundra Books,
1998. Alan Dingwall has a traveling companion, Norbert, an alien
who lives in Alan's nose—spaceship and all. Alan and Norbert talk
to each other and with Norbert's help, Alan deals with the bullies
at his middle school and even converts one.

Sheldon, Dyan. *My Brother Is a Superhero*. Cambridge, MA: Candlewick Press, 1996. Adam Wiggins lives in the shadow of his older
brother Keith, a natural athlete who likes to pick on Adam and his
best friend, Midge. When three older boys start bullying Adam and
Midge, having a big brother turns out to be a very good thing. (P)

Shreve, Susan. *Joshua T. Bates*. New York: Knopf, 1997. Joshua feels
small as he moves up to fourth grade the day after Thanksgiving.
The rules for fourth grade are different from those for third grade,
and Joshua worries he won't have any friends. He changes his
clothes, hairstyle, and attitude in an attempt to impress the wrong
kids. (P)

Sinykin, Sheri Cooper. *The Shorty Society*. New York: Penguin Books,
1994. Seventh grade brings many changes for Drew Minardi, and
one is particularly hard to accept. Last year, Danny Greeson was

his best friend, but now Danny is five inches taller and spends most of his time bullying Drew about being short. (M)

Skinner, David. *The Wrecker*. New York: Simon & Schuster, 1995. Theo and Michael work together to "wreck" the class bully who has been intimidating Theo for years. (P)

Slaven, Elaine. Illustrated by Brooke Kerrigan. *Bullying: Deal with it Before Push Comes to Shove*. Toronto, ON: James Lorimer & Company, 2003. Nonfiction. Aimed at students, this highly illustrated booklet is excellent. It discusses all types of bullying and has quizzes and self checks to get the points across clearly. (M)

Spinelli, Jerry. *Loser*. New York: HarperCollins, 2002. Zinkoff, from first grade through sixth grade, is a loser by everyone else's standards, but he's much too busy and excited about life to even notice people making fun of him. (P)

————. *Maniac Magee*. New York: HarperCollins, 1990. Jeffrey Lionel Magee loses his parents when he is three years old and spends the rest of his life looking for a home.

————. *Wringer*. New York: Joanna Cotler Books, 1997. It's bad enough that Palmer has to endure the neighborhood bullies, but when he's expected to become a wringer of pigeons' necks at the town's annual Pigeon Day once he reaches the age of ten, he has to find a way to stop it.

Soneklar, Carol. *Mighty Boy*. New York: Orchard Books, 1999. Timid and shy Howard Weinstein is "small for his age," and he hears those dreaded words far too often as he enters fourth grade. When Eddie Gervinsky calls Howard "Mighty Wimp," Howard looks to his favorite TV superhero for strength. (P)

Strasser, Todd. *Help! I'm Trapped in My Principal's Body*. New York: Scholastic, 1998. Andy, Jake, and Josh decide something must be done to stop Barry Dunn from bullying the whole eighth grade class. Using the Dirksen Intelligence Transfer Sysytem (DITS), Andy trades bodies with Principal Blanco.

Verdick, Elizabeth & Marjorie Lisovskis. *How to Take the Grrrr Out of Anger*. Minneapolis, MN: Free Spirit Publishing, 2003. Nonfiction. This book provides ways to manage anger and avoid being a bully.

White, Ruth. *Tadpole*. New York: Farrar, Straus, & Giroux, 2003. In 1955, Carolina lives with her mother and three sisters. Their favorite cousin, Tadpole, is a constant visitor as he tries to escape his abusive guardian. (P)

Wilson, Jacqueline. Illustrated by Nick Sharratt. *Bad Girls*. New York: Delacorte Press, 2001. Ten-year-old Mandy, mommy's little girl with long blond braids and pink dresses, can't escape the girl bullies at school. Even her former best friend, Melanie, uses their old secrets against her. Then fourteen-year-old Tanya, a wild, punkish foster child moves in next door and becomes Mandy's trusted friend.

Zeier, Joan T. *Stick Boy*. New York: Atheneum, 1993. The summer between fifth and sixth grade, Eric's parents get a divorce. He and his mother move out of state and he grows six inches. After last year's harassment in a public school, his mother puts him a private, Christian school. When the bullying starts again, Eric decides to deal with it himself.

Chapter Five

Middle School,
the Peak Years, Grades 7 and 8

As students enter middle school, usually in a new building, they receive two orientations: one from the staff and one from the students. As adults with a different perspective, we are very aware of the staff's definition of orientation: how to get around the building, operate lockers, teacher expectations of student work and behaviors, teacher availability for conferences and extra help, explanations of the school calendar, class calendar, sports calendar, club possibilities. The orientation provided by the students differs greatly, teaching the newcomers their proper roles, and what they have to do to survive and not usurp any of the power already established by the upper-class students. The youngest grade in any building has no power, and next year when they have earned a little power, they will get to indoctrinate the "new years." The rookies have to learn the rules. Which of these two orientations would you cling to for daily survival?

In this transition to middle school, "a combination of bullying and pro-social behavioral strategies are used to establish and maintaindominance."[1] Bullying increases until everyone understands who is in charge and knows who are the popular people. A similar process happens the first year of high school. Those new to the environment must learn the established rules of the school's social order.

One middle school teacher defined middle school as hormones, bodies, and energy run rampant. Suddenly not having the right shirt, ball cap, skirt, sweater, or slacks becomes enough reason not to go to school. There are still those who dress at home and redress on the way to school. In addition, girls claim "rights" to a particular boy even if there hasn't been any personal communication. All these behaviors and the insecurities that go with them create a fertile environment for harassment. It is not a surprise that harassment peaks in middle school.

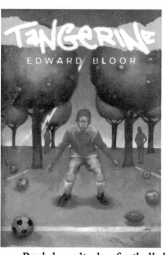

Edward Bloor, *Tangerine.*

Paul Fisher, his mother, father, and older brother Erik move into Lake Windsor Downs, an expensive new development in Florida. Paul will attend Lake Windsor Middle School, and his brother will be a senior and star kicker on the high school football team. It's part of the "Erik Fisher Football Dream" that Mr. Fisher sustains. The Fishers are a dysfunctional family; it is the year of a catharsis, the uncovering of secrets, and the start of healing.

Paul doesn't play football; he plays soccer even though he is visually handicapped from an accident of some kind when he was five, one of the family's secrets. Erik says Paul was too dumb to turn away from an eclipse and stared right at it. He calls Paul, "Eclipse Boy." Paul is afraid of his brother but doesn't really understand why. Too much of the past has been erased from his memory, but flashbacks are starting to provide clues. Despite this stress, Paul earns a spot on the soccer team, playing goalie until the school pulls him because of his disability. The one thing that belongs only to Paul gets taken away.

The land is as much a character in this novel as any of the people. It had been the tangerine center of the state. The new housing development where Paul's family moves is built on plowed citrus trees, and the unstable ground produces muck fires, mosquitoes, termites, and sinkholes. Lightning strikes this area more than any other place in the United States. Fall is the rainy season. One day the rains do not stop, and the seventh and eighth grade out-buildings are sucked into a huge sinkhole. Paul helps rescue several students. There are only minor injuries, but the buildings are destroyed. The students have to be accommodated elsewhere. Paul transfers to Tangerine Middle School, and never mentioning his handicap, goes out for the soccer team, the War Eagles. Tangerine Middle School, a poorer school where minorities make up most of the school population and many families work in the citrus business, is a tough school filled with kids fighting for survival. Paul holds his own and makes some friends, finding a way to belong. He delights and works hard in his new community, particularly on the soccer team. There he quietly builds a reputation of being willing to do as Coach Bright requests. The team leaders, Victor Guzman and Tino Cruz, accept Paul as a team equal.

At Lake Windsor High School, Erik is making his mark on the football field. He consistently kicks 40–50-yard field goals. He also picks up Arthur Bauer for his thug. Erik bullies Paul and his Hispanic friends for the fun of it and goes after others for revenge.

There are other signs that Erik cannot control his rage, but Paul, too frightened to confront Erik or tell his parents, files the knowledge away with the other secrets. The flashbacks are coming too frequently for Paul to ignore. One provides the truth about Paul's eyes. Erik and his friend trapped Paul and sprayed paint into his eyes. Their parents don't want Paul to hate his brother, so they have never talked about it. They sealed the event and have ignored every other sign of Erik's violent behavior.

By the end of the book, Erik and his thug have been caught with stolen goods from homes in their neighborhood and implicated in the death of a Hispanic man. The Erik Fisher Football Dream goes POOF!

This book is about many things, but mainly it's the story of a family held hostage by a bully. The younger brother is the primary target. Because neither is given the help needed, lives are ruined, potential lost, and trust betrayed. Inaction supports the crime.

Activities/Topics for Discussion

- How do Mr. and Mrs. Fisher treat Paul and Erik differently?
- Compare and contrast the two communities of Tangerine and Lake Windsor. What preconceived ideas do they have of each other?
- Why is Paul able to cross over those differences and find a place at Tangerine Middle School while his friend Joey is not? Explain.
- The Fisher family and the Cruz family are very different. Why is the Cruz family a stronger unit?

- Antoine and Shandra Thomas secretly play for different schools; Paul and Erik Fisher openly play for different schools. How can that be explained? Why is it allowed?
- List all the secrets in this book. Start with the Fisher family but expand to other families and the communities.

Quotes for Reader Response

- "Hey, Eclipse Boy, how many fingers am I holding up?" (33)
- Paige and Tina want to date football players, so these two will do. Erik and Arthur want to date cheerleaders, so these two will do. (39)
- I'm still afraid of Erik. I'm afraid of Arthur now, too. But today I wasn't a coward, and that counts for something. (84)
- The coach said to us, "You stand here by me, all of you. And stand up straight. Don't let some fool make you bow your head." (116)
- "Listen, Fisher Man, here it is. . . . If you're a War Eagle, then you're a War Eagle. You got brothers to back you up. Nobody's gonna mess with you, not anyplace, not anytime . . ." (121)
- *Forget it . . . Erik can't laugh this off. Erik can't leave this humiliation behind him. Someone has to pay for this. I'm not sure why I'm sure. But I am. Someone has to pay for this.* (129)
- "It was great to meet you, Erik. . . . And it was great to meet you, too, Paul." Mom, Dad, and Erik all pulled back at once, as if in group shock, as if that was the craziest thing they had ever heard. (176)
- "This is where it happens. This is where losers act like losers and winners act like winners. This is where they send some fool out here to punch you in the face. If you retaliate, you're playing their game. If you get focused on soccer, you're playing your game." (186–87)
- Erik pointed to us and spoke with mock admiration. "Look at this. I think it's great that these farm-labor kids get to spend a day away from the fields." (198)
- Arthur reached Luis, turned, and whipped the blackjack around with a loud *whack* against the side of Luis's head. Luis's arms shot up to cover his head as he staggered to the right. . . . Arthur stuck the blackjack back into his gym bag and continued walking, as if nothing had happened. (205)
- "Am I such a stupid idiot fool that I stared at a solar eclipse for an hour and blinded myself? Is that who I am? Am I that idiot?" (256)

- He [father] shook his head sadly. "We wanted to find a way to keep you from always hating your brother."
  I answered, "So you figured it would be better if I just hated myself?" (257)
- "Do you realize, Mom, that I've never been anything but a nerd? And now I'm going to enter this nerd school, not as a fellow nerd, but as a feared and notorious outlaw?" (289)

Sharon G. Flake,
The Skin I'm In.

Maleeka Madison defines herself, "I'm the darkest, worsedressed thing in school. I'm also the tallest, skinniest thing you ever seen." (4) Everyone notices and everyone lets her know they notice, particularly her dark-black skin and her poorly sewn clothes. But Maleeka and her mom are surviving as best they can after her father's death in a car accident. The first two years after he died, Mrs. Madison was lost in grief; now she spends her days teaching herself to sew. She makes all of Maleeka's clothes.

The new English teacher, Miss Saunders, has a huge white mark across half of her face. Maleeka says it looks like someone threw acid at her. The students are no easier on Miss Saunders than they are on Maleeka. The first day of school, Charlese Jones announces, "I sure ain't looking at that face forty-five minutes every day. No way." (7) Charlese calls the shots at McClenton Middle School. A while back, after a particularly humiliating scene on the bus, Maleeka offered herself to Charlese for protection. She would do all of Charlese's homework and run errands for her if Charlese would keep the worst of the harassment away. The only problem is Charlese is the biggest bully in school. Now Charlese feels she owns Maleeka.

Miss Saunders doesn't back down like Maleeka; she comes to teaching from a successful career in advertising. Her clothes are expensive and her confidence is secure. She wants to try teaching because she has decided it is time to give something back. A strong disciplinarian and an inspiring teacher, she challenges students with her high expectations.

Maleeka doesn't know if she can trust this misfit teacher. She's having enough problems fitting in without all her attention. John-John continues to taunt her about her darkness. Charlese shortens the leash and has another girl start a fight with Maleeka. Thanks to Miss Saunders, Maleeka's punishment is to work in the office. Miss Saunders also visits Mrs. Madison and tells her that Maleeka is falling through the cracks, and the office job will keep her out of trouble.

In one of her lessons, Miss Saunders has her students write about being someone else—a teenager from the seventeenth century. Maleeka chooses to be a girl on a slave ship and starts writing a journal. This journal continues through the book, weaving with Maleeka's own journal, and helps her gain confidence and strength in herself as well as her writing.

But Charlese is never far away and continues to treat Maleeka like her slave. Her older sister and guardian, JuJu, visits school to talk about Charlese's failing grades, particularly in English. A loud confrontation in the office ends with JuJu threatening Miss Saunders' job. The next day, Charlese declares war on Miss Saunders, and Maleeka has to help. Her quiet refusal only angers Charlese more. After many threats, Maleeka meets Charlese and two other girls before school to destroy Miss Saunders' room. During the vandalism, the curtains catch fire. The other three escape, but Maleeka is caught by the janitor. She is suspended and has to pay $2,000 for damages. She refuses to admit anyone else helped.

Miss Saunders knows Maleeka has not done this alone, and she practically begs her to tell the whole story, but Maleeka only admits to her part. Charlese has frightened her into silence. Not until Miss Saunders brings the two together in her classroom does Charlese's ugly anger betray her, and she yells at Maleeka, "You ugly, stupid black thing." (166) Maleeka cannot hold back any longer and she explodes at Charlese and tells Miss Saunders that Charlese and the twins were the ones who destroyed her room.

These three are suspended, and Charlese's family decides that she should live with her grandparents in Alabama. The school believes Maleeka has been punished enough and shortens her suspension. She returns to school and Miss Saunders's English class—a much stronger and more confident person, no longer afraid.

Activities/Topics for Discussion

- Why does Maleeka make a deal with Charlese in the first place?
- How are Maleeka and Akeelma, the slave girl in Maleeka's story, alike? How did Akeelma help Maleeka?
- Compare and contrast the lives of Maleeka and Charlese.
- How did Maleeka and Miss Saunders each have to handle discrimination because of their skin?
- How does this book show that prejudice about skin color can exist within a race? Is skin color an issue for you and your friends?
- Miss Saunders asks the class what their face says to the world. Can you answer that? What does your face say to the world?
- How does Miss Saunders handle the harassment she gets from the students?
- Why was John-John so mean to Maleeka?
- Because Maleeka was treated badly by the kids at school, she made a deal with Charlese for protection. How did this change her situation?

Quotes for Reader Response

- She was a freak like me. The kind of person folks can't help but tease. That's bad if you're a kid like me. It's worse for a new teacher like her. (1)
- "Don't let that fancy name fool you," John-John butts in. "She [Maleeka] ain't nobody worth knowing." (2)
- He's [John-John] my color, but since second grade *he's* been teasing *me* about being too black. (4)
- You got to *go* along with Char if you want to *get* along with her. (12)
- "Maleeka, Maleeka, we sure want to keep her but she so black, we just can't see her." (14)
- He's half and half—got a white dad and a black momma. He's lucky. He looks more like his dad than his mom. (17)
- "It takes a long time to accept yourself for who you are." (19)
- "I want you to know what it feels like to live in somebody else's skin and to see the world through somebody else's eyes." (24)
- "It's not about color . . . It's how you feel about who you are that counts." (40)

- I didn't used to mind being this color. Then kids started teasing me about it. Making me feel like something was wrong with how I look. (41)
- You have to take a stand when things aren't right. (107)
- "Maleeka, forgive and forget. That's easier than dragging around anger like sacks of stone." (110)
- "Some of us is the wrong color. Some is the wrong size or got the wrong face. But that don't make us wrong people, now does it?" (119)
- John-John's always talking about how black I am. Well, I'm still the blackest thing in the school, and it was me that saved his butt today. (156)
- "Call me by my name! I am not ugly. I am not stupid. I am Maleeka Madison, and, yeah, I'm black, real black, and if you don't like me, too bad 'cause black is the skin I'm in!" (167)

James Howe, *The Misfits.*

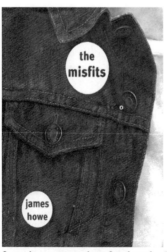

At Paintbrush Falls Middle School, seventh-graders Bobby Goodspeed, Skeezie Tookis, Joe Bunch, and Addie Carle have learned to survive with support from each other. Bobby Goodspeed lost his mother a few years earlier, and to cope with that loss and his father's depression and drinking, Bobby has started eating compulsively. Shortly after his mother's death, he began taking peanut butter and Marshmallow Fluff sandwiches, his mother's favorite, every day for lunch. He gets called Fluff, Dough Boy, and Roly-Poly. Addie Carle, who has been Bobby's best friend since before their memories started working, as their moms were best friends, is tall, thin, outspoken, and brilliant. She gets called Beanpole, Show-off, Big Mouth, Einstein, and Godzilla. They met Joe Bunch when they were four; he had just moved into Addie's neighborhood. Bobby knocked on

Joe's front door, and Joe opened the door wearing a dress, which he flipped up to prove he was a boy. Now Joe paints his pinkie fingernail, changes his name weekly, and gets called Faggot, Fairy, Queer, Tinkerbell, and Pervert. The three of them met Skeezie Tookis in kindergarten, but it took them until second grade to get past his bully, tough-kid image to form a friendship. Once he had friends, Skeezie stopped making trouble. He did, however, develop a fondness for black leather jackets, slicked-back hair, and haphazard personal hygiene, picking up labels like Greaser, Wop, Schizo, and Scuz. Others called them losers; they call themselves the Gang of Five (the fifth place is saved for any kid who needs somewhere to belong).

This year is an election year, and Paintbrush Falls Middle School has two political parties—the Democrats and the Republicans. Addie wants to form an independent party, and although they start one called the Freedom Party, they change it to the No Name Party. Their slogan is "Sticks and stones may break our bones, but names will break our spirit." Using the concept of teaser advertising, they put up posters around the school, each containing one of the names (Loser, Fag, Freak, Beanpole, etc.) they have been called, surrounded by a red circle with a red slash through it. Their campaign to stop the name-calling not only awakens the students but also the staff. The No Name Party does not win the election, but they do change the school environment.

Activities/Topics for Discussion/Writing

- All the names Bobby, Joe, Skeezie, and Addie have been called are listed on page 139. Go through the list and identify the ones you have also heard in your school. Add others that you have heard—or used.
- Make a private list of all the names you have been called. Look at that list and decide if any of those names really do fit you. Write a letter to yourself about how you feel about those names.
- What single word has power in your life, to change your mood, to make you angry, embarrassed, ashamed? Write a letter to Bobby or Joe or Skeezie or Addie about how that word can change a life.
- The Gang of Five spends considerable time cutting each other down. How is it different from when the other kids at school call them names?
- In chapter 7, Bobby talks about the size of his town and how it fits him. How well do you fit the size of your town?

- If you had to run for an office in your school, what would be your slogan?
- On page 123, Skeezie, Joe, and Bobby are remembering their early years. Skeezie remembers when they were little and had to walk holding a buddy's hand, and some lady going by saw Skeezie and Joe holding hands and thought they were "the cutest things." Then he says, "If you and I were walkin' down the street now and we were, y'know, holdin' hands like back when we were buddies in first grade, nobody'd say we were cute. They'd call us fags. Or do somethin' even worse. What's up with that?" Can you answer his question?

Quotes for Reader Response

- But all I can say is that if you are willing to dig below the surface, you will discover the real Skeezie Tookis, and there you will find as big a heart as was ever produced by the little town of Paintbrush Falls, New York. (2)
- Names come Addie's way, too, only in her case it is because of her being so tall, in addition to the factor of her intelligence, both of which fall on the plus side of the ledger if you happen to be a boy and are major liabilities if you were born into the world a girl. (11)
- As for Joe, well, he's been called more names than the world's most stinking umpire. (11)
- I wonder if maybe everybody gets names hung on them for only a little part of who they are. (13)
- Kids who are misfits because they're just who they are instead of "fits," who are like everybody else. (14)
- When you get down to it, thinking of somebody as 100% human seriously gets in the way of hating them. (46)
- I'm well on the way to totally betraying my lifelong friendship with Addie for the buzz I'm feeling from having actually made a certifiable popular person laugh with me and not at me. (84)
- DuShawn: That's so gay, y'know, weird.
  Addie: I hate that expression. Gay does not equal weird. (88)
- Skeezie: So does being cool mean you get to go around calling other people names? (91)
- I'm thinking there's a lot more to all of us than the names we're called or what we show on the outside. (121)

- This business of really knowing people, deep down, including your own self, it is not something you can learn in school or from a book. (124)
- It doesn't matter how many times I've been called names, it still hurts—and it still always comes as such a surprise that I never know how to respond. Or maybe I do, but I'm afraid. (131)
- "Sticks and Stones may break our bones, but names will break our spirit." (142)

Amy Goldman Koss. *The Girls.*

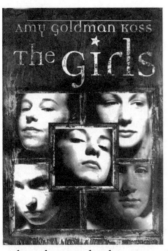

The novel is told in five separate voices, one for each of the main characters in alternating chapters. Maya, Renee, Darcy, Brianna, and Candace have their own middle school insiders group. Candace, the leader of the clique is self-confident, power-happy, beautiful, and admires others who are beautiful. She needs to be the center of attention and constantly keeps the group's focus on her. Darcy is small, thin, and insecure, and she worships Candace and works very hard to prove that she is Candace's best friend. She follows Candace's slightest request. Brianna, an aspiring actress, is pretty secure and the most likely to question Candace's whims. Renee, a thoughtful girl struggling with her parents' break-up, has a conscience that sometimes keeps her from enjoying the activities of the group. Maya, a kind, sweet-natured girl, is thrilled to be included in the group, having just transferred from another school.

They do everything as a group of five—until Candace decides that she is bored with the usual members. Maya is the first to go, and each of the others has to choose between following the leader or standing against her. Maya had given up all her old friends to belong to Candace's clique and did not have any warning that she was being dumped. Maya's father has arranged to take Maya and her little sister to Six Flags, Magic Mountain. They each get to invite a friend; of course, Maya calls Candace first. Her line is busy so Maya tries another group member and finds out from a mom that they are all on their way to Darcy's for a sleepover.

Darcy has no problem with Candace's decision to revoke Maya's membership; she didn't see why Candace had invited her to join in the first place. But she knew Candace did things like that, found someone interesting and asked her to join the group only to tire of her later. Brianna tells Candace and Darcy that she doesn't understand what happened, but she does not hate Maya. Candace takes aim; Brianna will be the next to go. Renee joins Brianna and together they find Maya in the cafeteria, and over lunch, clear up the "misunderstanding." While they eat, they look across the room and see Candace talking with Nicole, and Darcy looking very nervous.

Activities/ Topics for Discussion

- At the beginning of the book, did you think it would be fun to be part of this group?
- The five girls have very different definitions for friendship. Make a chart and write each of their names at the top of a column. Underneath, cite examples from the book showing how they each treat friends.
- Which of these five would you want for a friend? Why would you choose that girl?
- Evaluate the author's description of how these girls act. Is the book realistic? Do girls really treat each other like this? Do boys?
- Pair each girl with her mother. How are each mother and daughter alike? Different? How does each mother influence her daughter? Do they hold the same values? Look at yourself and your parent of the same gender, or the parent most involved in your life. How are you two alike? Different? Do you share the same values?
- Choose some passages that truly show each girl's personality. Give a dramatic reading.
- Do such cliques operate in your school? What do you think of them? Would you like to be in one? Why?

Quotes for Reader Response

- How long had they been planning to leave me out of whatever it was they were doing today? The grayness curled around my head, squeezing. (4)

- Candace struck a pose and in a regal English accent said, "But of course, the chorus would simply never do. It's the starring role or nothing for me!" She smiled as if she were kidding, but I don't think she was. (16)
- I didn't know how everyone else felt about Candace's games, but I thought they were tests, like walking on hot coals or something, to prove how tough we were. (28)
- I had to exorcise my room, purge it of ghosts, chant cleansing incantations, burn incense, light candles—do something to get those girls out of there. I needed to reclaim my room. Make it mine and only mine. (37)
- Now that Candace had decided I was no longer worthy, did any of them give me another thought? (39)
- It was almost as if Candace were the queen, condemning Maya to death, and Darcy was the one who carried out the order. The executioner—an executioner who loved her work. (43–44)
- What did it matter what the other girls thought of her [Maya]? It only mattered what I thought, right? (46)
- I shuddered, imagining myself having to walk into school with everyone hating me. I wouldn't be able to do it. If I were her, I'd run away. (48)
- "The point is that I did not raise my daughter to be a bully. I need you to explain your actions toward Maya." (58)
- "Darcy," she said in her stiff lawyer voice. "You and your pals did not invent cruelty and exclusion. It's been going on since Eve. But it is the work of small minds." (58)
- I could barely whisper when I said, "I don't even know, really, why everyone's so mad at her."
  "We're not mad at your little friend. . . . We just think she's boring." (80)
- "Brianna's next, huh? It should be your turn in no time." (85)
- Me and the other girls thought about Candace constantly, trying to keep her happy. But I suspected that Candace never really thought about us. We were just there, like the air. (87)
- Until Candace had turned against me, I'd felt nothing about Maya being dumped, except that it wasn't my business. Why had I thought that? Of course it was my business, I was supposed to be her friend! (103)

By John Lekich

John Lekich,
The Losers' Club.

Alex Sherwood, permanently disabled by cerebral palsy, gets around on crutches, which earns him a few privileges. One, he has a pass to travel through the halls when they aren't crowded with students. Two, a mixed honor, is that Jerry Whitman, the school's golden boy, teachers' pet, and extortion ringleader who fondly calls his targets, "Jerry's Kids," does not demand cash from him. Because of it, Alex is a type of safe zone for these kids. They actually argue over who gets to sit near him, walk beside him, eat lunch with him, and some even call him "Savior Sherwood." In addition to offering this safety zone, Alex also makes loans to kids who don't have enough money to pay off Jerry. Because Alex is one of them, these loans are always repaid with a small interest: all of this goes into the loan fund and the cash keeps circulating. Oddly, some unity grows out of this situation: the boys have accepted the seemingly true fact that they are losers and have started the Losers' Club, which meets once a week at Winston Chang's mansion. They even have their own club room with a Jerry Whitman dartboard. Soon they have to screen applicants because there are so many.

Alex has two close friends: Winston Churchill Chang and Rubert "Manny" Crandall. Winston's father, a highly successful businessman, moved his family to Vancouver a few years earlier, but most of his business is still in Hong Kong where Winston's parents spend 99.5 percent of the year. Winston and his older brother, Neville, live in the family mansion with Cola, the family's Doberman. However, Neville is in California competing in a big Karaoke contest, so Winston lives with only Cola. As one of Jerry's Kids, Winston has no problem with his weekly protection fee; however, he suffers at Whitman's hands in another way. Winston is very short, and Whitman's thugs stuff Winston into his locker for the fun of it. Winston keeps a pillow in there because it happens so often. Because of the frequent rescues, Winston has bonded with Mr. Winecki, the school janitor who kindly removed the top shelf in Winston's locker to give him the room a growing boy will need. Manny calls the diminutive Winston "the Short One." Winston calls Manny "the Fat One."

Manny Crandall has a quick wit and a great sense of humor, which help him handle the "fat" harassment at school, but only his friendships with Alex and Winston help him handle his loneliness at home. His judgmental father, new wife, and baby live in posh Manhattan where Manny used to live until the divorce. His dad rarely calls. Now Manny and his mom, a chronic alcoholic, live in Vancouver in a small apartment. Manny is the cook, housekeeper, and caregiver.

Alex also lives alone, but he loves it, admitting that he is "addicted to freedom." Mr. Crandall, whose inventions are advertised on late-night TV infomericials, is presently hiding out from a very threatening dissatisfied customer. Afraid that the home phone is tapped, he always uses the code name "Uncle Vito" when he calls in. Mr. Crandall's fears are not unfounded, and when Alex realizes that someone is watching their apartment, he decides to accept Winston's offer and moves into the mansion.

At school, the daily routine progresses as usual, until one day Jerry pushes Alex too far and suddenly a challenge has been made in the form of the Christmas Festival of Lights Contest. If Alex's team wins, Jerry will end his extortion ring and stop bullying everyone. If Jerry wins, Alex has to close down the Bank of Sherwood and swear to never help or hang out with another loser ever again. As the preparations begin, a few adults step in to help: Harry Beardsley, Winston's neighbor who goes through a personal transformation thanks to Alex, Winston, and Manny; Mr. Sankey, a wise and gentle man who is also superintendent of Alex's apartment building; and Winston's janitor friend, Mr. Winecki. These healthier father role models come from unexpected places.

Of course, Alex and the Losers' Club win the competition and start to believe that being losers may not be their life avocation. Although this book is filled with humor, the element of kids' labeling and acceptance of themselves as losers, consequentially furthering the bullies' long-range damage, is very serious. However, the bonding in the Losers' Club provides the support and sense of belonging they were denied at school, and enables them to stand up to the bullies—and beat them with Christmas lights.

Activities/Topics for Discussion

- "Whitman, who has a very warped sense of humor, began calling his extortion victims 'Jerry's Kids.'" (6) That is warped. Why?
- What is "running the gauntlet"?
- Julie shows Alex the strength that exists in Loser Power. Define that strength.
- Why was Harry Beardsley called "the Beast"?
- Compare and contrast the three fathers: Mr. Sherwood, Mr. Chang, and Mr. Crandall.
- Compare Harry Beardsley, Mr. Winecki, and Mr. Sankey.
- Watertank is in an awkward position: He hates to hurt kids, but he is Jerry's collector. Why do you think Watertank took this job? How does it make him feel about himself? What will his younger sister think when she finds out?
- By the end of the story, what understanding do we get of Jerry Whitman?
- Use a crystal ball to predict the future for Alex, Manny, and Winston.

Quotations for Reader Response

- Manny likes to call himself an activist for the horizontally challenged. His motto is, "I'm wide and I'm here." (7)
- If there's one thing Whitman knows, it's how far to push a loser. He usually leaves your borderline losers alone. (8)
- If I had to rate who was the most popular target in the school, it would have to be Winston Churchill Chang. (9)
- The flying doughnut trick sounds more complicated than it is. Simply put, it is Jerry throwing a stale cafeteria doughnut at the loser of the day. (30)
- Manny says he often racks his brain to figure out why Jerry Whitman is so evil. He finds it especially perplexing since Jerry's family is the type you see pictured on boxes of granola. The Whitmans are what you might call terminally wholesome. (60)
- "The Losers' Declaration of Independence" it began: "Give us your nerds, your geeks, your hard-core losers yearning to break free from the tyranny of Jerry Whitman Jr.!" (66)
- For your average loser with a dysfunctional family, the Yuletide season is a major sore point. (85)

- Manny says that since we have never been even remotely cool, we have no understanding of how important it is to hang on to your cool status. (95)
- "You know something, Sherwood?" said Jerry, "You've got *spirit*. The trouble is, your kind of spirit is bad for business. It's got a way of making losers think they aren't losers at all." (101)
- "I think it's worth the risk," I [Alex] said. "Besides, I don't want to back down."
  "Why not? We're losers. Backing down is what we *do*." (106)
- "If we are to keep our freedom, we must allow Jerry and the boys to maintain a decent level of abuse."
  That is the way losers think. (146)
- "There are far more losers in the school than there are Jerry's boys," said Julie. "Harness the raw power of losers and you can do practically anything." (202)
- Call it Loser Pride. After years of cowering in corners, we could be open about who we were. We had a *project*. We had a *goal*. We were still losers, of course, but nobody was going to put us down. . . . We could be ourselves. (225)
- "What's wrong, Manny?"
  "What *isn't* wrong?"
  "Pick something we can change." (233)

David Lubar,
Hidden Talents.

Martin Anderson carries one weapon: his mouth. Words fly out of this eighth-grader's mouth like a repeating rifle, and they always find their mark. After being expelled from three middle schools, Martin sits in a bus delivering him to Edgeview Alternative School, wondering if he will make all the staff hate him there too.

Martin's roommate, Torchie, has a problem with fires, although of course he doesn't admit it. Cheater always gets A's on all his work, but no one believes it. Lucky has a stash of all kinds of goodies in his room, but he says he never steals anything. Flinch just cannot seem to settle down, and he is always roaming like a caged animal. Trash trashes things, mostly by throwing them across the room. Martin fits right in.

But not all the students are as welcoming as Martin's friends. Bloodbath and his two sidekicks, Lip and Grunge, rule the school. Martin finds out the first day when they initiate him with a punch to the stomach. Doubled-up on his side, his bullying words don't do him any good. Bloodbath is a whole new level of bully.

Martin's first day of classes go about as expected. He uses sarcastic remarks as a shield against attacks and to establish his reputation, only he uses those remarks against the teachers. He wins, and they almost all hate him by the end of the day. Later he finds out they are the ones who evaluate him and decide when, or if, he can leave Edgeview.

But Martin is not dumb. As he watches his friends, he observes some interesting things. Trash doesn't really throw anything; things really do seem to move by themselves. Torchie doesn't even carry a functioning lighter. Flinch can play dodge ball like he has radar. And Cheater finishes other people's thoughts. In the library, Martin starts researching psychic abilities. Flinch has precognition, Cheater is telepathic, Torchie is telepyric, and Trash is telekinetic. These guys are gifted!

They don't see it that way. All these words sound like another way of saying that they are crazy—and none of them wants to wear that label. Eventually, with the help of science experiments, they accept their gifts and try to learn how to live with them. Even Martin's ability to find the words that will hurt someone the most can be turned around, he can also find the words to validate someone.

At the same time, word gets out that the school may be closed. While Bloodbath wants to help that happen, Martin and crew have suddenly found something to hang on to. They put their hidden talents to work trying to stop Bloodbath's sabotage. When Bloodbath hides twenty candles connected to M-80s, Lucky finds some, but Torchie concentrates and extinguishes the flames. When Bloodbath and his sidekicks have a planned rumble, they suddenly discover their shoelaces tied to their chairs, thanks to Trash. When the evaluators randomly select a student to interview and Martin's file is picked, he can answer their questions without his standard defensive attack.

All turns out well. Bloodbath and his buddies are transferred to a restrictive unit; Martin and his friends adjust to success. Martin, on the bus again, returns home after realizing his father was the first bully in his life. Things will not be easy, but Martin does have his hidden talent.

Activity/Topics for Discussion

* Martin does not seem to use his sarcasm with his friends; he saves it for adults. On his first day, he uses it on each of his teachers. What have the teachers done that trigger Martin's defense?
* On page 99, Martin realizes that Torchie "was actually stumbling through life totally unaware of his abilities." Most of us do that. Make a chart. On one side list your potentially negative behaviors; on the other side of the chart, across from each behavior, state it as a positive quality. For example, I can be very stubborn, which can be a very negative behavior, but it also means people can't easily push me into doing things, which can be very positive.
* When Martin tries to convince Torchie that he is telepyric, Martin gets frustrated and says, "If you were smart, you'd believe me. But I guess you're not very bright. Face it—you're probably not even smart enough to be called stupid." (100) Does Martin really believe this statement will help him convince Torchie of his ability? Why does Martin resort to his sarcasm?
* Sarcasm can make people laugh, but it almost always hurts someone. Why is sarcasm considered witty?
* Why do the boys refuse to believe they have hidden talents? What are they afraid of?
* How is Mr. Briggs, the science teacher, different from the others on the staff?
* If you were a bully in your school and got sent to an alternative school with lots of bullies, many more powerful than you, how would you survive?
* There is an old saying, "Consequences are a pain and they go on for a long time." How does this prove true for Martin?

Quotes for Reader Response

* He [Bloodbath] seemed like the sort of kid who'd hurt his friends as quickly as he's hurt anyone else. I figured the best thing to do was to let him think I was a spineless wimp who'd stand there and take whatever he did to me. (20)

- Bloodbath lashed out and hit me in the stomach. As his fist shot into my gut and drove all the air out of my body, I bent over, then crumpled to the floor. (21)
- "If enough people call you crazy, maybe you begin to believe it, even it you aren't." (33)
- I liked dodge ball. There's a wonderful satisfaction in smacking someone nice and hard with a fairly harmless ball. (50)
- I realized that Bloodbath was sort of like a human version of a stealth bomber—he could slip in, cause pain, and slip away without detection. (56)
- "I don't want to be different." (135)
- "People hate anyone who's different." (145)
- "You [Martin] have a gift. You know how to hurt someone. You know how to dig deep and hit a nerve." (200)
- "Your power is pretty obvious," Cheater added. "Once we figured it out, it was really amazing watching you in action." (201)
- The look on his face—it was the look of a bully who was about to do damage. It was the look of a bully about to feast on pain. . . . I was jolted by Bloodbath's expression. I'd seen that same look so often on my father's face. The face of a bully. (208)
- "I almost can't blame my dad for hating me." I gasped as my own words sunk in, squeezing my chest into a tight knot. For a minute, I couldn't talk. I'd never admitted that particular truth before. (210)
- The last thing I want is to be a bully. Not all bullies use their fists. Some use words. (213)

Sue Mayfield,
Drowning Anna.

Anna Goldsmith wasn't like just any new girl in school. She was smart and beautiful, spoke perfect French, played center forward on the girls' hockey team, won awards as a violinist, and spoke with a classy accent from the south of England. At thirteen, she seemed more confident and sophisticated than most students in her school.

The book opens with a crying Anna preparing to kill herself. She carries her journal, her mother's anti-depressants, and a bottle of vodka into the bathroom and locks the door. No one will be home for hours; she has plenty of time—to die. We learn what has led to this point through three channels: flashback from the point of view of Anna's friend, Melanie; Anna's mother who sits beside her hospital bed watching her comatose daughter; and Anna's journal. The flashbacks are woven with the present happenings in the hospital room where she lies in an alcohol-induced coma, with her mom beside her, reading Anna's journal, which brings Anna's voice into the book. The journal and Melanie's flashbacks give a full accounting of Anna's torment. She was not imagining it; Melanie saw what Hayley did to Anna.

On the first day Anna attends school, Hayley Pankin claims her. They are inseparable by the end of the first week. Hayley, a very wealthy, privileged, and popular girl, likes being the center of the school. No one wants to offend Hayley. Her smile seems like a reward, and to be included in her circle of friends means instant popularity. But Hayley also drops people and then turns everyone else against her victim. Such is what happened to Anna. She and Hayley dressed alike, spent all their time together, shared all secrets—and then Hayley started ignoring Anna—no arguments, no explanation, no dramatics—just one day around Easter time, Hayley stopped being Anna's friend. After that there was nothing that Anna could do right!

At first Hayley simply ignores Anna, moves her seat to the other side of the room, mimics Anna behind her back—and the teachers'. Anna, truly confused, doesn't know what is happening and still tries to talk to Hayley, who retorts with sarcasm and put-downs. Then Hayley starts verbal attacks to Anna's face, calling her names, making fun of her accent, her good-girl image, her grades, and her body. Hayley knows all of Anna's insecurities, and she now uses them to hurt Anna. If a teacher overhears Hayley, she says she was just kidding or Anna was being overly sensitive.

Hayley's attacks turn physical. Melanie sees Hayley purposely hit Anna's ankle with her hockey stick during a game. One time Melanie sees her trip Anna; another time Hayley uses a balance beam to pin Anna against the wall. Each time Hayley claims it was an accident or Anna's clumsiness. The adults never really see what is happening; Hayley is very subtle.

Not until Anna's mother discovers that Anna has started cutting herself do her parents get involved. Mrs. Goldsmith talks to the administrators, who agree to discuss the issue with the teachers. The girls would be separated, moving Melanie with Anna so she will have a friend. Hayley's parents refuse to believe that their daughter could behave in such a way. The teachers are confused because both girls had been such close friends only last year, and Anna has always been so self-assured. The new restrictions help for a while, but then things return to what they were. Hayley, quietly seething, comes back with a vengeance. Anna convinces herself she just has to ignore the harassment. Her mom and dad assume all is well because she answers all of their questions evasively.

Hayley realizes her best way to continue manipilating Anna is through Melanie, so she courts Melanie by including her in gatherings, inviting her on vacation trips, and tricking Melanie into revealing secrets about Anna. Melanie is caught in the middle and feels tremendously guilty, but she still cannot seem to turn away from Hayley's attention. For Anna, it is the final betrayal. As she is drinking the vodka, she writes letters to her parents, Melanie, and Hayley. Melanie delivers Hayley's letter, who reads it and shows absolutely no response.

At the hospital, Anna's heart goes into a rhythm disturbance, a heart attack—but she survives.

In writing this book, Mayfield does not ease up for a second. The intensity will stay with you for hours after you finish the last page.

Activities/Topics for Discussion

- In this book, girls do all the bullying, not the boys. How do girls bully differently than boys?

- Why is it difficult for the adults in the book to believe that Anna was the victim of bullying? What about her keeps her from fitting the image of the typical bully's victim?
- What are some of the things that Hayley did to taunt and humiliate Anna?
- Create a character analysis of Melanie. What is her part in the bullying? How is her betrayal the final blow in Anna's destruction?
- List all the people who had a part in Anna's deterioration. Explain how each was involved.
- Name three people Hayley manipulated besides Anna and Melanie. How were they used against Anna?
- Reread the three suicide letters Anna wrote. What message was she hoping to express in each?
- Explain the meaning of the book's title and the poem it is from.
- The teachers and staff did not see what Hayley was doing to Anna. Who could have helped?
- Could this happen in your school?

Quotes for Reader Response

- People—kids in our class—try to keep "in" with her [Hayley]. It's been like that since we started school. It's better to be in her gang than out of it. (17)
- Hayley Parkin does that. She starts things and then other people get the blame. (20)
- Hayley . . . had never been more friendly. It didn't dawn on me that she was only being friends with me to get at Anna. I was stupid enough to think she liked me. (51)
- When people talk about bullying you think of gangs. Helpless victims. People being beaten up. . . . The teachers reckon our school doesn't have a bullying problem. They think that by our age we've grown out of "that sort of thing." (109)
- The trouble with Hayley and Anna was it was all so discreet, so undercover, so subtle. . . . None of us would have called it bullying. Not then. (109)
- I saw Hayley bring her stick down like an axe, against Anna's ankle. Anna yelled and dropped her stick. (115)
- Then it was messages. Scruffy bits of paper handed around the class. Furtive. Childish. *Anna Goldsmith needs liposuction. Anna Goldsmith is a slag. Anna Goldsmith was dumped.* (116)

- I heard Ruth Smith say to Joshua, "That was sick, what Hayley said to Anna. She's being a real cow these days!"

  The next day Hayley got Siobhan to slap Ruth's face in the cloakroom. Hayley was standing by, watching, "Just watch who you're calling a cow, Ruth!" (137)
- I think Hayley's behavior was really grinding her [Anna] down. She didn't say much. She'd got much quieter, less outgoing, as if she wanted to blend into the background. As if she wanted to become invisible. (138)
- Guilt is a terrible thing. It eats at you, chews your insides. I [Melanie] couldn't settle. I kept hearing my own words in my head, pounding around and around like fists on a drum. (174)
- *Afterward, as the blood started to congeal, it throbbed. I didn't mind the pain. It was bearable because I had caused it. I had done the damage. I wasn't just the victim. It made me feel powerful. For once it was me that was controlling something.* (209)
- *Why haven't they noticed? Why can't they see what's going on? Why can't they stop it?* (213)
- What the teachers don't know, and what the Parkins choose not to see, is that Hayley Parkin is devious. She's sly. She manipulates people. People are shit scared of her. (231)
- Even in elementary school she could control other kids. There, it was more blatant. She made rings around people in the yard—linked hands with other children and trapped victims inside the circle. Then she'd taunt them. You can't get out! I bet you can't get out! (231)
- Suddenly Hayley was behind me. She grabbed a handful of my hair and yanked it backward. I froze. She pulled harder till my scalp was smarting. Then she dug her nails into my arm and said, "If you go running to Mummy again, Anna, I might get really nasty." (242)

JERRY SPINELLI

Jerry Spinelli, *Stargirl.*

On the first day of eleventh grade, Leo Borlock hears everyone talking about her. The school is abuzz about a new student named Stargirl. Then he sees her in the lunch room, dressed in a long ruffled ivory outfit, maybe her grandmother's wedding gown, a ukulele strapped to her back, and carrying a bright sunflower-covered canvas bag. She strolls around the lunch table, strumming her ukulele and happily singing, "I'm looking over a four-leaf clover." High school students cannot handle this type of eccentricity.

At first Hillari Kimble, self-appointed Queen Bee, believes Stargirl is a trick the administration hopes will stir up some school spirit. This girl is just too different to be real. In each class, she daily decorates her desktop with a tablecloth and knickknacks, sings happy birthday to people she doesn't even know, and wears stranger costumes everyday. She does nice things for everybody—from the shiest to the most popular. She treats everyone the same, she treats everyone as though she liked them.

For one of the football games, Stargirl plays her ukulele with the band, huddles with the football team, and cheers with both sets of cheerleaders. The cheerleaders ask her to join them, but they didn't understand—Stargirl cheers for everyone.

Basketball season starts out fine, but as Mica Area High School starts winning game after game, the fans do not like her cheering for the other team. Stargirl got in the way of their newfound school spirit. The fans turn against her, and when the team loses in the championship playoffs, Stargirl is an easy scapegoat. They say that she demoralized the team.

While all this is happening, Leo Borlock falls in love. He finds Stargirl enchanting but confusing, so he goes to see Archie, A. H. Brubaker, a retired paleontologist who still teaches school for those who drift into his home. To this professor of life, Leo talks about Stargirl. Archie reveals that he has been teaching her for a few years, and he believes that she is one of the originals, a very real person. Though Leo is wonderfully happy in their relationship, he still can't quite define Stargirl.

The students at school are not having any trouble defining Stargirl—she is simply too weird. Everyone starts ignoring her, and as Leo travels with her, he also becomes invisible. Archie calls it shunning. Stargirl seems not to notice; Leo can't seem to not notice. When he explains the shunning to Stargirl, she disappears for a little while returning as Susan, Miss Typical-Teen. She has matched her clothes, her speech, and her behaviors to those of the other girls. Leo thinks he will be happy, but Stargirl isn't. The shunning continues, and Stargirl realizes before Leo, that they didn't like her when she was herself; they do not like her when she tries to fit in. She can't win, so why play? Stargirl lets Leo go. And with a miserable sense of relief, he leaves. Archie had asked him one question, "Whose affection do you value more, hers or the others?"

But on the night of the Ocotillo Ball, Stargirl wows them all. She arrives in the sidecar of a bicycle covered with a flower blanket. Dressed in a bright yellow dress with a sunflower on one wrist, Stargirl steals the show. She asks the band director to play the bunny hop and soon she is leading ten people, twenty people, fifty people, two hundred people all over the dance floor and then out the door and onto the golf course. The music never stops, and neither do they. The few left behind wait impatiently, till someone spots the jiggling, hopping human chain return—still on beat. That is her last dance; when she returns her sidecar is waiting and off she goes, never to be seen again.

Leo had missed the dance and his last chance to see Stargirl. He commiserates with Archie, who tells Leo that she had loved him so much that she had tried to change for him, to be like everyone else, but she couldn't. "Star people are rare." (177)

Activities/Topics for Discussion

- At first the kids at school don't like Stargirl, and then they do, and then they don't. Why this changing acceptance?
- The bullying in this book is shown in the shunning and the pressure to conform. For Stargirl, changing herself was harder to accept than the shunning. Explain why she stopped trying. What would you do if you were in Stargirl's place?
- Hillari is really the unofficial leader of the student body; why is she so upset by Stargirl?

- Page 19 says that Wayne Parr "was the grand marshal of our daily parade." Why was he the leader? How had he earned this? What does that say about the student body at Mica Area High School?
- Why the name "Stargirl"?
- On page 28, Leo says, "We honored her by imitation." They were honoring Stargirl. Why is this ironic?
- If only one person was going to be with you from your birth to your death, how would you treat that person? Who is the only person who can be with you from your birth to your death?
- Stargirl and Archie have some similar eccentricities. Why is Archie accepted and respected while Stargirl is shunned?
- How would Stargirl be treated at your school? Why?
- Archie asks Leo, "Whose acceptance do you value more, hers or the others?" (104) Whose acceptance do you value most?

Quotes for Reader Response

- We wanted to define her, to wrap her up as we did each other, but we could not seem to get past "weird" and "strange" and "goofy." Her ways knocked us off balance. (11)
- She had no friend, yet she was the friendliest person in school. (15)
- Because she was different. *Different.* We had no one to compare her to, no one to measure her against. She was unknown territory. Unsafe. We were afraid to get too close. (26)
- "On the contrary, she is one of us. Most decidedly. She is us more than we are us. She is, I think, who we really are. Or were." (32)
- All of her feelings, all of her attentions flowed outward. She had no ego. (53)
- "How did this girl come to be? I [Archie] used to ask myself. Sometimes I thought she should be teaching me. She seems to be in touch with something that the rest of us are missing." (102)
- "Whose affection do you value more, hers or the others?" (104)
- I had never realized how much I needed the attention of others to confirm my own presence. (126)
- I [Leo] knew exactly what I had done. I had linked myself to an unpopular person. That was my crime. (132)
- If it was up to me, I wouldn't change a thing. You're fine with me the way you are. But we're not alone, are we? We live in a world of them, like it or not. (138)
- I realized now that the shunning would never end. And I knew what I should do. . . . I should show Stargirl and the world that I

wasn't like the rest of them, that I appreciated her, that I celebrated her and her insistence on being herself. But I stayed inside. (165-6)

- "Star people are rare. You'll be lucky to meet another." (177)

Carol M. Tanzman, *The Shadow Place.*

Lissa Sontag and Rodney Porter have lived next door to each other all their lives, playing and fighting like sister and brother. Now fourteen, Rodney is breaking apart from all the years of living with a raging father. Only Lissa knows all the parts, and she is sworn to secrecy.

Rodney has grown up in a constant atmosphere of pain and criticism. Deeply connected to his mother, he has felt abandoned since the divorce. She never calls him; the drinking had cost her her family. His father, a verbally abusive bully to her and his two sons, has lost all of them as well. Mr. Porter, a baseball coach, favored his elder son, Jared, a natural athlete who has escaped to college. Jared never calls or comes home. Rodney now has all of his father's attention, and he does not weather the family dysfunction as well without his brother's presence. A sensitive artistic boy who had bonded deeply with his mother, he has grown to hate his father. His mother and Lissa are his two strongest connections, and now Lissa is all he has left.

At school, short on social skills and the right image, Rodney lives on the edge of Lissa's circle of friends, who tolerate him because of Lissa, but that is changing. As Soo Young tries to impress Jared, she uses their mutual irritation of Rodney as a bonding opportunity. The group forces Lissa to eliminate Rodney from the lunch table and attending school events with them. Lissa hates doing so—but she does. At school Rodney and Lissa hardly talk, though at home they still manage a fractured friendship.

As Rodney becomes more outcast at school, he starts thinking of revenge. Maybe he can't get back at his father, but he might be able to teach the boys at school a lesson. Through an on-line chat-room, Lissa discovers that Rodney is trying to buy a gun. She uses a fake profile and screen name to get in the chat-room, and Rodney unknowingly confides his loneliness to her. At the same time, his mother re-enters his life. Sober and working an Alcoholics Anonymous program, she has remarried and wants to see Rodney before she and her new husband leave for his new job in Saudi Arabia. Rodney believes that she will take him with her. When she visits and Rodney has his suitcase packed, she obviously has not thought about taking him with her. Lissa, hiding on the other side of the backyard fence, watches it all unfold.

Abandoned a second time by his mother, Rodney surrenders to his anger—at her, his father, his brother, the kids at school, and himself. He disappears with a handgun and a rifle. Lissa, paralyzed by her promise not to tell and by her fears of what might happen, pieces together all that she knows. She saw him at school with a gun; she also saw him on the roof in their neighborhood with the gun aimed at his father, and now in the last e-mail message to her fake screen name, he has hinted he is going to kill himself. At midnight she races through the neighborhood canyon until she finds him. Alone, desperate, on the edge, he holds the gun and pushes her into his hideaway. The adult in each of them argues over facts and circumstances; the child in each of them just argues like sister or brother. It is that old comfortable pattern that connects them, and Lissa convinces Rodney that if he kills himself, his father wins. As Rodney cries, Lissa slowly lifts the gun away from him.

Activities/Topics for Discussion

- How is Rodney a product of his home environment? Use all three of his family members in your explanation.
- How does Rodney's home life affect how he behaves at school?
- Mr. Parker is a rageaholic. Using what you know about the word and what you know about Mr. Parker from the book, explain what rageaholic means. (Check the Internet for Rageaholics Anonymous.)
- Lissa's group at school tells her they don't want Rodney near them and Lissa has to tell him. What would you do if you were in the same position?
- Lissa's aunt tells Lissa's secret because she thinks it's cute. Lissa keeps Rodney's secret because she promised. When is telling a secret the right thing to do?

- Have you ever let someone else decide who you could have for friends? Have you ever told your friends who they could have for friends?

Quotes for Reader Response

- "Fine. How much do you hate your father?"

  Rodney's smirk vanished. He stared, transfixed, into a place only he could see.

  "As much as anyone can hate anyone." (6)
- But he [Mr. Porter] didn't smash his fist into Rodney's jaw. Instead, he let the baseball fly. It whizzed past Rodney's ear, *blam*, and hit the wooden fence so hard a slat cracked in half.

  "Pick it up, boy," ordered Mr. Porter, eyes narrowed to angry slits.

  "Now!" (10)
- Not a single word was said to Bob Porter. No one interferes with the "best coach" in the league. (20)
- "You've got to tell him. And he can't eat lunch with us any more, either. That's why I called. I just got off the phone with Jared. He wants you to talk to Rodney tonight." (42).
- Gary laughed, "What a loser!"

  "Why can't you guys lay off?" Lissa sighed. "He's not eating with you, so who cares what he wears?"

  Jared threw a lettuce leaf at her. "Aren't you tired of defending him, Lissa? He's an asshole, and if you can't see it, you're an asshole, too." (52)
- What choice did she have? She *had* to dump him. If not, she'd be eating lunch alone or with Rodney—while her former friends snickered at her. (54)
- Why couldn't she stand up for him? Why not just say, *I'm eating with Rodney whether you guys do or not.* Or even say, *You're acting like spoiled brats—he can eat with us if he wants.*

  It should have been easy. (127)
- She saw him. *Really* saw him, standing alone, nearly in the same spot as in her dream.

  Rodney!

  There it was, a gun, an actual gun, raised with both arms and aimed straight at the stage! (156)
- "Life is not a courtroom, Lis. You need proof to convict, not to go to your parents if you're worried about a friend." (162)

- "You see how he treats Rodney, but you ignore it. Everyone ignores it! All the yelling and humiliation, bossing him around and . . ." (164)
- "You know . . ." Rodney lifted his teary, muddy face. "You're the only human who's ever listened to me. My whole life. Not my mother, not Jonah, not . . . anyone." (176)
- "You won't be alone. Come back with me, Rodney. Someone will help you get to eighteen. I swear. . . . It's my turn, I dare you to believe I'm telling the truth." (178)

Doug Wilhelm, *The Revealers.*

Russell Trainor, Elliot Gekewicz, and Catalina Aarons find each other, as teens who are bully targets often do. Russell is Richie Tucker's favorite target, for no other reason than that he's available and Richie now considers Russell as his property. Catalina has recently moved to the U.S. from the Philippines. Her mother, a Filipina, married her father, an American businessman on assignment in the Philippines. Bethany rules the seventh-grade girls, and if she doesn't like Catalina, nobody likes Catalina. And Elliot Gekewicz is the "one kid it's okay for anybody, absolutely anybody, to trash." (17)

In an attempt to explain her history to other students, Catalina writes an open letter about how she came to be at Parkland Middle School and posts it on the school's KidNet, a self-contained network for the students. Inspired by Catalina's courage, Elliot writes up and posts his last experience with his harassers, who dangled him by his feet over the side of a bridge and then let go. Soon other kids start sending their stories in to this trio, who post them on KidNet under the heading of "The Revealer." One teacher likens it to an underground newspaper.

As more students send in personal stories for everyone to read, the school climate starts to change and the bullies start to feel threatened. There are even some stories from students who confess to being a bully and wish they could take it back. One letter accuses Bethany of forcing the writer into doing her social studies project. Bethany's father, an attorney, shows up and accuses "The Revealer" staff of slander. The principal, Mrs. Capelli, who is frightened by technology and public opinion, has been looking for a way to close down KidNet. With this posting in "The Revealers," she has her excuse. KidNet is shut down.

Russell, Elliot, and Catalina try one more thing. They enter the Creative Science Fair with a computer program, "Welcome to the Bully Lab." They have researched the problem of bullying at Parkland Middle School. The main menu offers, "I. Hypothesis, II. Research Methods, III. Research Project, IV. Video Reenactments, V. Video Interviews, VI. Gallery of Nasty Notes, VII. The Stories." (183) Several students have helped create the reenactments and interviews. The whole student body fills out research questionnaires. Everyone loves the project, including the judges, who so thoroughly praise Principal Capelli, that she agrees to reopen KidNet.

At the end of the book, Catalina has made some friends in spite of Bethany's power. Elliot has learned to stand up for himself and feels a lot less like a dork. Russell and his bully, Richie Tucker, have come to a friendly understanding and acceptance of each other. They have even helped each other fight some other demons.

Russell, Elliot, and Catalina, definitely dynamic characters, have turned their lives around through their support of each other.

Activities/Topics for Discussion

- Before starting the book, have a class discussion about bullying in your school. Later create a survey similar to the survey used in the book on page 185. Give it to as many students as possible to fill out. Compile the results. Write an article for the school newspaper.
- Bethany DeMere, Richie Tucker, and the Jock Rots (Chris Koppell, Jon Blanchette, and Burke Brown) represent different bullying styles. What behaviors does each use? How are these alike? How are they different? What is the one goal that they have in common?
- Examine the relationship between Russell and Richie. How does it start out? What is it like at the end of the book? What changed the relationship?
- What are Principal Capelli's views on bullying in Parkland Middle School? Is this view typical of most administrators? Most teachers?

- Read the letter on page 145. By the end of the book, we know that Bethany has written that letter to get "The Revealer" in trouble. How does that letter prove that Bethany knows exactly how to bully?
- Sometimes people have a difficult time understanding when something is bullying and when it is just kids having fun. Discuss ways to tell the difference. (One good guideline is that if the behavior would be illegal if it happened to adults, it is probably bullying.)
- The book talks about Anne Frank and the world during her life. Name some bullies in history. What happened to them? Are there any bullies in powerful positions in the world today?

Quotations for Reader Response

- "Let me tell you how it is, little *boy*. This is not over, okay? This is never over. Every time you turn around—you better be watching for me. Okay, little boy? Because you're mine now. You are *mine*." (7)
- If you have no hope of being accepted in a cool clique, or any clique for that matter, you're safest if you can manage not to get noticed at all. (10)
- You know how there's always . . . one kid who it's okay for anybody, absolutely anybody, to trash.

  In our school, that last kid was Elliot. . . . I wasn't sure why he was the one, but the fact was that in Parkland School seventh grade, no matter who you were, Elliot Gekewicz was lower on the social scale than you. (17)
- Bethany DeMere is the ruler of the top clique of seventh-grade girls. She's popular; and she's one of those people who knows just what to say to cut you down. A lot of times she doesn't say anything—she just looks away and shakes her head so her hair ripples down her back. . . . Of course, to her I did not exist. I didn't even have hair-shaking status. (28)
- I couldn't help wondering if the only way I would ever get to be somebody in seventh grade was by getting myself brutalized. (51)
- "Girls at this age can be really vicious, and so vulnerable. I almost think it's more serious business than you boys with your physical stuff." (68)
- "I mean, if a few people persecute somebody, most of us pretend it isn't happening, right? We don't want to see it." (86)

- "I used to think it meant something bad about me, that she [Bethany] acts that way," she [Catalina] said. "Now I think a person like that just needs someone to plot against. She needs enemies." (128)
- "You're a nobody who suddenly thinks you're a somebody. You and your friends. But that doesn't give you the right to say nasty things about me or anybody else."

  "Huh," I said. "So what gives you that right?" (131)
- "I still don't understand why you'd want to hurt somebody that way," Catalina says. "But I finally decided if I let you get away with it, you'll think nobody will ever stand up to you. You'll think you can control everything. I realized it was worth taking a risk to prove what's really true." (191)

Annotated Bibliography

Selected Short Stories

Avi. "Biderbiks Don't Cry." In *From One Experience to Another: Award-Winning Authors Sharing Real-Life Experiences Through Fiction*. Ed. by M. Jerry Weiss and Helen S. Weiss. New York: Forge, 1997. 203–20. Charlie's father urges him to fight his tormentors, but Charlie has a better, but riskier, solution.

Bagdassarian, Adam. "The Fight." In *First French Kiss and Other Traumas*. New York: Farrar, Straus & Giroux, 2002. 62–71. The conflict began with a collision in a basketball game in gym class and escalated from there, so Will has no choice but to fight Mike.

Brancato, Robin. "White Chocolate." In *Connections: Short Stories by Outstanding Writers for Young Adults*. Ed. by Donald R. Gallo. New York: Delacorte Press, 1989. 84–93. Wally disguises his anger and academic inadequacies by bullying his teacher, Ms. Loring.

Gantos, Jack. "X-15s." In *No Easy Answers: Short Stories About Teenagers Making Tough Choices*. Ed. by Donald R. Gallo. New York: Delacorte Press, 1997. 227–35. This kid will do just about anything to join the X-15s, and Simon, the gang's leader, makes a pretty bizarre demand.

Lubar, David. "Duel Identities." In *Lost and Found: Award-Winning Authors Sharing Real-Life Experiences Through Fiction*. Ed. by M. Jerry Weiss and Helen S. Weiss. New York: Forge, 2000.

15–33. Scott Tarbell becomes the butt of his classmates' jokes when he declares that his favorite sport is fencing.

Mazer, Anne. "The Transformation of Cindy R." In *Stay True: Short Stories for Strong Girls*. Ed. by Marilyn Singer. New York: Scholastic Press, 1998. 65–85. Looked down upon by her classmates, Cindy is transformed by her fairy godmother in this unusual twist on the Cinderella fairy tale.

Miklowitz, Gloria D. "Confession." In *No Easy Answers: Short Stories About Teenagers Making Tough Choices*. Ed. by Donald R. Gallo. New York: Delacorte Press, 1997. 99–111. Tired of being victimized by neighborhood gangs, Jim and his buddies strike back with disastrous results.

Peck, Richard. "Priscilla and the Wimps." In *Sixteen: Short Stories by Outstanding Writers for Young Adults*. Ed. by Donald R. Gallo. New York: Delacorte Press, 1984. 42–45. Monk Klutter and his stooges dominate the school until Priscilla puts Monk in his place.

Saldaña, René Jr. "Un Faite." In *Finding Our Way*. New York: Wendy Lamb Books, 2003. 67–74. With only a month to go before his family will move out of town, Kiko wants nothing more than to stay out of trouble, but it seems as if the *mochos* won't cooperate.

Salisbury, Graham. "The Doi Store Monkey." In *No Easy Answers: Short Stories About Teenagers Making Tough Choices*. Ed. by Donald R. Gallo. New York: Delacorte Press, 1997. 295–321. The guys just want to have a little fun with Randy, the retarded kid, until Smythe thinks maybe it's not so funny.

———. "Frankie Diamond Is Robbing Us Blind." In *Island Boyz*. New York: Wendy Lamb Books, 2002. 118–41. Everybody fears Frankie Diamond, king of the bullies, until they meet Lynette.

———. "Shark Bait." In *Ultimate Sports: Short Stories by Outstanding Writers for Young Adults*. Ed. by Donald R. Gallo. New York: Delacorte Press, 1995. 118–43. Looking as white as coconut meat, David Ford stands out from the rest of his new classmates in Hawaii, and so he gets picked on by nearly everyone, especially by Johnny Blas.

Strasser, Todd. "On the Bridge." In *Visions: Nineteen Short Stories by Outstanding Writers for Young Adults*. Ed. by Donald R. Gallo. New York: Delacorte Press, 1987. 122–28. Seth admires Adam's toughness, right down to his sleeveless denim jacket and the way he flicks his cigarette away, until Adam abandons Seth in a crucial situation.

Wartski, Maureen Crane. "A Daughter of the Sea." In *Join In: Multi-ethnic Short Stories by Outstanding Writers for Young Adults*. Ed. by Donald R. Gallo. New York: Delacorte Press, 1993. 86–96. When Lien, a Vietnamese immigrant, is the victim of racial slurs from the class bully during a biology class field trip, her previously distant classmates come to her support.

Werlin, Nancy. "Shortcut." In *On the Fringe*. Ed. By Donald R. Gallo. New York: Dial Books, 2001. 49–60. Lacey has to decide whether or not she will risk her own safety to warn Catrine about an impending attack by Will Brennerman and his nasty associates.

————. "War Game." In *Twelve Shots: Outstanding Short Stories About Guns*. Ed. by Harry Mazer. New York: Delacorte Press, 1997. 88–100. When Lije is victimized by bigger kids, his next-door neighbor and friend Jo just watches, but then reconsiders her lack of action.

Other Books

Some books are also appropriate for other levels. I-Intermediate, H-High School.

Anderson, Laurie Halse. *Speak*. New York: Farrar, Straus & Giroux, 1999. Melinda describes her freshman year in high schoo! following a summer when she was raped at a party and so traumatized that she can't talk about it. Assisted by a supportive art teacher, she slowly begins to give voice to her feelings. (H)

Bloor, Edward. *Tangerine*. San Diego: Harcourt, 1997. Paul Fisher lives in the shadow of his older brother, Erik. Legally blind, Paul still manages to play soccer while Erik steals the family's attention as a star football kicker. Slowly the truth about Paul's blindness comes out in flashbacks of cruelty involving Erik. (H)

Brugman, Alyssa. *Walking Naked*. New York: Delacorte Dell, 2004. Megan Twu is not only part of the eleventh-grade in-group, she leads it. If someone strays, she calls for an intervention. Then she gets put in detention with Perdita Wiguiggan, the school freak, and against every rule of her group, Megan starts to befriend Perdita. (H)

Byalick, Marcia. *Quit It*. New York: Delacorte Press, 2002. Last year, Carrie was a happy eighth grader, but over the summer she has developed Tourette's syndrome, and ninth grade becomes a nightmare. (H)

Carvell, Marlene. *Who Will Tell My Brother?* New York: Hyperion, 2002. Though Evan has always been conscious of his Mohawk heritage, it is not until his senior year in high school that he feels the need to take a stand. He does so by asking the school board to change the offensive Indian school mascot. His attempts are quiet and follow the established recourse, but the harassment he suffers ranges from personal verbal attacks to violence against his whole family. (H)

Cole, Brock. *The Facts Speak for Themselves.* Asheville, NC: Front Street, 1996. Linda, thirteen, has experienced too much loneliness and responsibility in her young life. She and her two younger brothers only survive their mother's reckless relationships because Linda fills the parent role. (H)

Cheripko, Jan. *Rat.* Honesdale, PA: Boyds Mills Press, 2002. When fifteen-year-old Jeremy Chandler testifies against the popular basketball coach for molesting a cheerleader, his relationship with the other students, particularly the team, is destroyed. The new coach challenges Jeremy to still do his best. (H)

Crowe, Chris. *Mississippi Trial, 1955.* New York: Phyllis Fogelman Books, 2002. While visiting his beloved grandfather in Mississippi, a white teenage boy meets Emmett Till, a feisty black teen from Chicago, who is soon murdered for whistling at a white woman. (H)

Dessen, Sarah. *Dreamland.* New York: Viking, 2000. After her older sister runs away from home, Caitlin gets involved in a relationship with a "hot," secretive, and very intelligent drug dealer who later becomes abusive. (H)

DiCamillo, Kate. *Tiger Rising.* Cambridge, MA: Candlewick Press, 2001. Rob Horton and his dad are trying to survive after his mother's death. Rob hates school, where he has to face the taunts of the other kids, but then he meets Sistine Bailey, who takes the taunts and fights back.

Flake, Sharon G. *The Skin I'm In.* New York: Jump At The Sun/Hyperion, 2000. Because Maleeka has dark-black skin, the other kids torment her. Miss Saunders, the new English teacher, has a white mark over half her face. Charlese doesn't let up on either of them.

Friel, Maeve. *Charlie's Story.* Atlanta: Peachtree Publishers, 1997. Charlie was abandoned by her mother at age four. Ten years later

the cruelty of her classmates who bully her because of that abandonment nearly causes Charlie to end her life. (H)

Friesen, Gayle. *Men of Stone*. Toronto, ON: Kids Can Press, 2000.
Fifteen-year-old Ben had a strong interest in dance but gave it up
because he was tired of the harassment. Claude's bullying is escalating, and Ben takes up boxing as a way to survive. (H)

Gallo, Donald R., ed. *On the Fringe*. New York: Dial, 2001. A collection of short stories written by well-known authors who specifically write for teens. Each story focuses on teens that are on the
fringe of acceptance. (H)

Griffin, Adele. *Overnight*. New York: Putnam, 2003. The Lucky Seven,
the best group in the sixth-grade, is having a sleep-over at Caitlin's
house. Gray, the quietest member in the group, worries about being
really accepted by the others. When Gray disappears, the reader
discovers each girl's inner thoughts as the search intensifies.

Hiaasen, Carl. *Hoot*. New York: Knopf, 2002. Roy Eberhardt has just
moved to Florida from Montana, and being the new kid isn't any
fun this time either. While dodging the middle-school bully, Roy
gets involved with Mullet Fingers, an older boy who lives in the
swamp and is fighting to save burrowing owls. (H)

Holt, Kimberly Willis. *When Zachary Beaver Came to Town*. New
York: Henry Holt, 1999. Toby Wilson thinks nothing exciting ever
happens in Antler, Texas, until his mom wins a chance to sing at
the Grand Ole Opry, his best friend's brother writes home from
Viet Nam, and Zachary Beaver, the fattest boy in the world, comes
to town. (I)

Howe, James. *The Misfits*. New York: Atheneum, 2001. Four social
outcasts in seventh grade create a third political party and run for
student council on a platform of "No Name Calling."

Kimmel, Elizabeth Cody. *Visiting Miss Caples*. New York: Dial, 2000.
During a school project in which she has to read to an elderly shut-
in, Jenna and Miss Caples help each other face painful aspects of
their lives as Miss Caples' past parallels Jenna's present.

Klass, David. *You Don't Know Me*. New York: Farrar, Straus &
Giroux, 2001. Although fourteen-year-old John says nobody
knows the first thing about him, his multilayered thoughts amusingly reveal everything we need to know about his painful
life—algebra class, band practice, involvement with girls, and his
home life, especially his abusive stepfather. (H)

Koja, Kathe. *Buddha Boy*. New York: Frances Foster Books/Farrar,
Straus & Giroux, 2003. Justin doesn't plan on befriending the

weird new kid who calls himself Jensen, but after seeing how others at wealthy Edward Rucher High School treat this newcomer with a shaven head, kind smile, and gentle ways, Justin can't go along with the crowd. (H)

Koss, Amy Goldman. *The Girls*. New York: Dial Books, 2000. Middle school cliques can be very cruel, and Koss shows one from the inside. Powerful Candace decides who is in and who is rejected according to her whims. Told in the voices of five members of the group in the beginning of the book, we see what happens when Candace tires of one.

Lekich, John. *The Losers' Club*. Toronto, ON: Annick Press, 2002. Jerry Whitman and the other "haves" make life miserable for the "have-nots" at Marshall McLuhan High School. Alex Sherwood, dubbed Savior by the Losers' Club, has cerebral palsy and walks with crutches.

Lubar, David. *Flip*. New York: Tor, 2003. When Ryan finds several disks that aliens left behind, he is able to transform himself into various legendary characters (Babe Ruth, Spartacus, Gandhi) that help him deal with Billy Snooks, the school bully.

———. *Hidden Talents*. New York: Tor, 1999. At Edgeview Alternative School, Martin and his odd friends discover that they have special abilities that get them into trouble, but when controlled, can be used for positive purposes—like handling the school bullies. (H)

Lynch, Chris. *Gold Dust*. New York: HarperCollins, 2000. In 1975, Richard Riley Moncrief knows the world would work better if he were in charge. Richard befriends Napoleon, a new student from the Dominica, who feels the discrimination that Richard doesn't.

Mayfield, Sue. *Drowning Anna*. New York: Hyperion, 2002. Thirteen-year-old Anna Goldsmith moves to a town and a new school where Hayley chooses Anna to be her new best friend. Things are wonderful, until Hayley drops Anna. Told in flashbacks after Anna has tried to kill herself, this book weaves together Anna's journal, her mother's bedside watch, and the reflections of her friend, Melanie. (H)

Mazer, Norma Fox. *Out of Control*. New York: Avon Books, 1993. Rollo Wingate thought his life was perfect because he had two best friends, but following his friends leads Rollo into bullying and harassment. This book gives us an inside view of both the bully and the target. (H)

McNeal, Laura, and Tom McNeal. *Crooked.* New York: Knopf, 1999. Clara has a crooked nose; Charles and Eddie Tripp have crooked lives. Things get complicated in ninth grade when bad, crooked things start hurting good people. (H)

Mikaelsen, Ben. *Touching Spirit Bear.* New York: HarperCollins, 2001. Ordered to participate in a Native American Circle of Justice program as an alternative to jail, Cole is banished for a year to a remote island in Alaska where he is mauled by a huge white bear. (H)

Muharrar, Aisha. *More than a Label.* Minneapolis, MN: Free Spirit Publishing, 2002. Nonfiction. Muharrar was still in high school when she wrote this book, but it isn't an English class assignment. She compiled her research from more than one thousand Teens Label Surveys and wove that information with her thoughts—which are pretty down to earth. (H)

Oates, Joyce Carol, *Big Mouth and Ugly Girl.* New York: Harper-Collins, 2002. Matt Donaghy, a.k.a. Big Mouth, and Ursula Riggs, a.k.a. Ugly Girl, develop an unlikely friendship after Matt is wrongly accused of threatening the school with a bomb and Ursula is the only one who stands up for him. (H)

Philbrick, Rodman. *Freak the Mighty.* New York: Scholastic, 1993. Max, bigger than most kids his age, gets called "Stupid" and "Dummy." Freak, tiny and sickly, is brilliant. With Freak on Max's shoulders, they can take on the world. (H)

———. *The Last Book in the Universe.* New York: Blue Sky Press/Scholastic, 2000. In a future time without hope, Spaz tries to rescue his little sister with the help of Ryter and a proov (genetically perfected) girl who lives in Eden. (H)

Plum-Ucci, Carol. *The Body of Christopher Creed.* San Diego: Harcourt, 2000. When a schoolmate disappears, most of his peers offer insensitive opinions of why and what happened. Slowly the pain of Christopher Creed's life and the way he was bullied begin to emerge. (H)

Rapp, Adam. *The Buffalo Tree.* Arden, NC: Front Street Books, 1997. Thirteen-year-old Sura struggles to survive his six-month sentence in a juvenile detention center with a particularly sadistic inmate. (H)

Romain, Trevor. *Bullies Are a Pain in the Brain.* Minneapolis, MN: Free Spirit Publishing, 1997. Nonfiction. With practical guidelines and cartoon-like illustrations, this book is a necessity for students, teachers, and parents. (I)

————. *Cliques, Phonies, & Other Baloney*. Minneapolis, MN: Free
Spirit Publishing, 1998. Nonfiction. With the same format as *Bullies Are a Pain in the Brain*, this book suggests ways to avoid the
cliques and create meaningful, healthy friendships. (I)

Scrimger, Richard. *The Nose from Jupiter*. Toronto, ON: Tundra
Books, 1998. Alan Dingwall has a traveling companion, Norbert,
an alien who lives in Alan's nose—spaceship and all. Alan and
Norbert talk to each other, and with Norbert's help, Alan deals
with the bullies at his Middle School and even converts one. (I)

Shaw, Susan. *Black-eyed Suzie*. Honesdale, PA: Boyds Mills Press,
2002. Abused by her mother, twelve-year-old Suzie closes herself
into an imaginary box. While recovering at a hospital, Suzie must
deal with her mother's bullying and that of another patient, Karen,
who both picks on Suzie and defends her. (H)

Sinykin, Sheri Cooper. *The Shorty Society*. New York: Penguin Books,
1994. Seventh grade brings many changes for Drew Minardi, and
one is particularly hard to accept. Last year, Danny Greeson was
his best friend, now Danny is five inches taller and spends most of
his time bullying Drew about being short. Other shorties, Bo and
Kate, join Drew to even the score.

Skinner, David. *The Wrecker*. New York: Simon & Schuster, 1995.
Theo and Michael work together to "wreck" the class bully who
has been intimidating Theo for years. [This book is out of print but
recent enough that many libraries have it.] (I)

Slade, Arthur. *Tribes*. New York: Random House, 2002. After the disappearance of his father, Percy escapes into the safe analytical
world of science as he studies the different tribes in his high
school: the Jock Tribe, the Born-Again Tribe, the Grunge Tribe,
and others. (H)

Slaven, Elaine. Illustrated by Brooke Kerrigan. *Bullying: Deal with it
Before Push Comes to Shove*. Toronto, ON: James Lorimer &
Company, 2003. Nonfiction. Aimed at students, this highly illustrated booklet is excellent. It discusses all types of bullying and has
quizzes and self checks to get the points across clearly. (I, H)

Spinelli, Jerry. *Stargirl*. New York: Random House, 2000. A new student named Stargirl celebrates her uniqueness in eccentric ways
that stun the students of Mica High School. (H)

————. *Wringer*. New York: Joanna Cotler Books, 1997. It's bad
enough that Palmer has to endure the neighborhood bullies, but
when he's expected to become a wringer of pigeons' necks at the

town's annual Pigeon Day once he reaches the age of ten, he has to find a way to stop it.

Strasser, Todd. *Help! I'm Trapped in My Principal's Body*. New York: Scholastic, 1998. Andy, Jake, and Josh decide something must be done to stop Barry Dunn from bullying the whole eighth-grade class. Using the Dirksen Intelligence Transfer Sysytem (DITS), Andy trades bodies with Principal Blanco. Hilarity reigns in this sci-fi attempt to rid the school of its bully.

Tanzman, Carol M. *The Shadow Place*. Brookfield, CT: Roaring Brook Press, 2002. Lissa and Rodney have lived next door to each other for years. She's been his only friend through his parents' divorce, his mother's abandonment, his father's abuse, and now the bullying at school. Can she save him from himself?

Tullson, Diane. *Edge*. Toronto, ON: Stoddart Kids, 2002. After joining a group of misfits, ninth-grader Marlie Peters has to decide if belonging to a group is worth giving up what one believes is right. (H)

Verdick, Elizabeth and Marjorie Lisovskis. *How to Take the Grrrr Out of Anger*. Minneapolis, MN: Free Spirit Publishing, 2003. Nonfiction. This book provides ways to manage anger and avoid being a bully.

Weaver, Will. *Farm Team*. New York: HarperCollins, 1995. Billy Baggs loves baseball and has a wicked pitching arm at fourteen, but while his dad is in jail, he has to run the family farm and his mom must get a job. The baseball coach sees Billy pitch and gets him on the team with all the town boys. (H)

Wilhelm. Doug. *The Revealers*. New York: Farrar, Straus, & Giroux, 2003. Russell, Elliot, and Catalina have nowhere to go for help with the harassment each is enduring, until they band together and post the discrimination on the school's KidNet.

Wittlinger, Ellen. *What's in a Name*. New York: Simon & Schuster, 2000. The voices of ten different students in Scrug Harbor High School give the reader a more complete view of hidden motivations and hurt feelings than even these characters have. (H)

Woodson, Jacqueline. *Miracle's Boys*. New York: Penguin Putnam, 2000. Three brothers, Ty'ree, Charlie, and Lafayette, try to survive after their mother's death. But since Charlie has come back from Rahway prison, he's changed: He's Newcharlie now. (H)

Yamanaka, Lois-Ann. *Name Me Nobody*. New York: Hyperion, 1999. Emi-lou and Yvonne have grown up together, best friends, self-adoptive sisters, closer than family. But suddenly growing up is more like growing apart. The diversity of the islands and the language add to the story which is set in Hawaii. (H)

Young, Karen Romano. *Video*. New York: Greenwillow, 1999. An assignment for Whole Learning class requires eighth graders at Lincoln Middle School to observe someone and take notes in a log. Janine can't think of anyone more interesting than herself, never realizing she is the class bully. (H)

Notes

1. Pellegrini, Anthony D. ""The Roles of Dominance and Bullying in the Development of Early Heterosexual Relationships." In *Bullying Behavior: Current Issues, Research and Interventions.* Ed. By Robert A. Geffner, Marti Loring, and Corrinna Young. (New York: The Haworth Maltreatment & Trauma Press, 2001).

Chapter Six

Hazing, Bashing, and Sexual Harassment, Grades 9–12

High school is not easy. For the first time, the statistics in students' files will follow them to college. Add to that the pressure of trying to fit in without being too obvious. Alhough bullying behaviors have peaked in middle school, class hazing, sexual harassment, and gay bashing take on new dimensions in high school. Everyone new to the school— class, team, or club—faces some form of initiation. Most are mild, but others range in intensity from intimidating to dangerous. Dating becomes more serious, and some relationships seem more like marriages, as ownership is involved. In the hallways, groups are still checking each other out; hands and words grab; rumors build and destroy reputations with a new severity. Just like in middle school, the need to belong dominates. Only a few are strong enough to remain unattached, and they are labeled as loners, eccentrics, or outcasts. As in earlier grades, the elite continue to rule with the enabling ignorance of the adults in the building. Homophobia grows stronger, whether out of lack of education, cultural fears, or the threat to one's status within a group. Academic harassment, socioeconomic harassment, racism, religious harassment, profiling—whatever exists in the world, exists in high school. And this is our last chance to influence these students' thought patterns.

Books in this chapter have high school-aged characters. If the annotation is labeled M it means that the book is accessible for high school students and more sophisticated middle school readers. If a book is listed here without the M designation, I have made a judgment call based on the issues presented. You may disagree and will make your own judgment based on your knowledge of the student to whom you hand the book. When in doubt, read the book first.

Laurie Halse Anderson. *Speak.*

Melinda Sordino is a heroic character. A popular, secure, hardworking eighth grader with an active circle of friends last year, she enters high school as a complete outcast, her pain as achingly vivid as her chewed bottom lip. Last year's friends only talk to her in whispers behind her back. Completely exiled from human compassion, either invisible or the center of a bull's-eye, Melinda never speaks.

Slowly Anderson reveals Melinda's history. She called the police to an end-of-the-summer drinking party, and because someone found her dialing 911 and alerted the crowd, everyone believed she had turned them in. But Melinda called because she had been raped by a senior male. By the time the police arrived, everyone had left and Melinda was home showering and burying her secret deep in silence. Three weeks later, she entered the ninth grade still in the shutdown of shock.

The book deals with several levels of harassment/bullying. Melinda suffers the sexual harassment of the rape, and then the social ostracism for being perceived to be a snitch. Even her best friends believe that she betrayed them and that she has earned her punishment.

Then there is Heather, new from Ohio. She tries to establish herself in her new school, and hopes that by connecting with Melinda she will find a clan to belong to. Heather's search for a group to join and the treatment she endures to qualify for membership showcases the relational aggression tactics so prevalent with girls.

At school, with her parents, alone, and in public, Melinda is silent. She only invests herself in her art. Her art teacher, Mr. Freeman, a sensitive and eccentric man, has assigned her "tree" for her year's theme. An old janitor's closet becomes her private hideaway, and she defines that space with posters, quotes, and art. Slowly she works at reconstructing herself.

Eventually she and her attacker, Andy, cross paths. She is terrified, but then Melinda discovers that Rachel Bruin, her former best friend, has started dating him. Melinda tries to warn her, but Rachel thinks Melinda is just jealous. One day in frustration and anger, Melinda writes, "Andy Evans—a guy to stay away from" on the bathroom wall. Other girls sign on in agreement, giving Melinda the validation that she badly needs.

At the end of the book, Andy traps Melinda in her closet and she is able to do what she wishes she had done last summer—she fights him. Hitting back and screaming for help, she escapes, straight into the arms of the women's lacrosse team, armed with their sticks.

Abandoned by so-called friends, withdrawn from her parents, Melinda battles out of her victimization and begins healing herself. The theme from "Rocky" should be playing as you finish the book. Melinda Sordino may very well be the most courageous and heroic character you will ever encounter in literature.

Topics for Discussion/Writing

- This novel is so well titled. List all the images Anderson creates around Melinda's silence and her slow return to speech.
- Using quotes from the book, describe how other students at school treat Melinda.
- David Petrakis belongs to the Cyber-genius clan. Why doesn't he get bullied?
- How do Melinda's parents contribute to her isolation?
- How does Melinda's behavior contribute to her isolation?
- Heather wants to join the "Marthas" clan. What is that group's reputation? How are they identified? What must Heather do to become a member?
- Compare Mr. Freeman, the art teacher, with Mr. Neck, the social studies teacher, in their treatment of students.
- Andy Evans is a bully. Why does his "bad guy" reputation make him attractive to girls?
- According to the bathroom wall, many girls know that Andy Evans is bad news. Why is it only whispered or written secretly inside toilet stalls? Why doesn't someone say it to his face? Why do some girls ignore the warnings?
- Describe how Melinda's hidden feelings are revealed in her artwork.

- How do the developing phases of her art project, the tree, parallel the phases of Melinda's recovery?
- In this book, Melinda and Heather are both targets of a type of bullying. Who or what helps each of them leave that role?

Quotes for Reader Response

- Her eyes meet mine for a second. "I hate you," she mouths silently. She turns her back to me and laughs with her friends. I bit my lip. I am not going to think about it. (5)
- I'm getting bumped a lot in the halls. A few times my books were accidentally ripped from my arms and pitched to the floor. I try not to dwell on it. It has to go away eventually. (14)
- I need a new friend. I need a friend, period. Not a true friend . . . just a pseudo-friend, disposable friend. Friend as accessory. Just so I don't feel and look so stupid. (22)
- The same boys who got detention in elementary school for beating the crap out of people are now rewarded for it. They call it football. (29)
- I pull my lower lip all the way in between my teeth. If I try hard enough, maybe I can gobble my whole self this way. (39)
- Mostly I watch the scary movies playing on the inside of my eyelids. (50)
- "Freshmeat." That's what IT whispers. IT found me again. I can smell him over the noise of the metal shop and I drop my poster and the masking tape and I want to throw up and I can smell him and I run and he remembers and he knows. He whispers in my ear. (86)
- I wonder if Hester tried to say no. She's kind of quiet. We would get along. I can see us, living in the woods, her wearing that A, me with an S maybe, S for silent, for stupid, for scared. S for silly. For shame. (101)
- Why can't I scream, say something, do anything? Why am I so afraid? (161)
- I unlock the front door and walk straight up to my room, across the rug, and into my closet without even taking off my backpack. When I close the closet door behind me, I bury my face into the clothes. . . . I stuff my mouth with old fabric and scream until there are no sounds left under my skin. (162)
- I'm fighting the shock of having a guest [Heather] in my room. I almost kick her out because it's going to hurt too much when my room is empty again. (177)

- The time has come to arm-wrestle some demons. (180)

Catherine Atkins, *Alt Ed.*

In America, society seems to sanction the harassment of two types of people: gay people and overweight people. Our schools are no exceptions. Homophobia, a complex fear particularly in the adolescent world, results in behaviors ranging from name-calling to violent physical attacks. The bully sees no difference between someone who is gay and someone who is perceived-to-be-gay. Media and fashion influences which define "perfect" with the newly created size zero, complicate the adolescent female's (and male's as well) fears about her body. The judgments exist inside her head and in the thoughts of those around her. To be fat translates to being ugly, being unacceptable. Body image equals self image.

When ninth-grader Susan Calloway's mother died three years ago, her family lost its center. Mom had been the heartbeat for her husband, a coach at the local high school, and her two children, Susan and Tom, a year older. After her death, each turned away, no one was ever home—even when they were all there. With her mother's chubby frame and an eating compulsion that she uses to try to fill up this new hole in her life, Susan stumbles into high school fat. Baggy black jeans and rotating mock turtlenecks become her school uniform. Chants of "fat, fat, ugly fat" and pig oinks follow her through the halls.

Brandon Slater has been labeled gay and rumors change daily. Hate talk, messages scribbled on his locker and on desktops, trash phone calls, and shoves in the hallway make his life at Wayne High torturous. A petition signed by 273 guys who refused "to share a locker with Brandon Slate the Faggot" hangs in the boys' locker room.

Kale Krasner loves his truck maybe even more than he loves to trash talk fat girls and gay guys. One day when Brandon has reached his tolerance level for the harassment, the hate mirrored from Kale's hate drives him to act. Brandon doesn't take a gun to school or a knife to his wrist—he scratches and spray paints Kale's truck. Susan watches and silently cheers Brandon's attack on their tormentor. The two are caught and assigned to a new alternative-to-suspension program, twelve weekly sessions with Mr. Duffy, the school counselor, and four other students on the brink of suspensions: Randy Callahan, Tracee Ellison, Amber Hawkins, and, of course, Kale Krasner.

As the group starts, Mr. Duffy is the only one who is upbeat. Tension, resentments, and defenses fill the room. Slowly each teen reveals buried truths and shares the pain of unwelcomed actions and words.

Randy Callahan seems to be an all-around good guy, but for too long he has been just an observer, watching the harassment and condoning it with his silence. Susan has a crush on him. The day her mother died, Susan and her brother, Tom, fled to the park where they found Kale and his friends about to torture a kitten. Randy, his brother, and their father helped rescue the kitten, and Mr. Callahan took Susan and Tom home. Tracee Ellison wears a silver WWJD bracelet, a nice beginning, but true faith takes practice and acts of acceptance. She judges people by stricter rules than she uses to judge herself and yet still gets caught up in trying to be perfect. Amber Hawkins has a tough reputation, and after Brandon, has probably heard the most sexual slurs. A strange mixture of passivity and aggression, she doesn't choose her battles well. Her hard, defensive exterior protects a very scarred and tender heart. Kale, with a small physique but a big bravado in cowboy hat and boots, has nearly no awareness of others as people. Lacking the human connectors that the other kids have, he is completely unable to put himself in anyone else's position—and therefore changes the least, if at all.

Susan hates Kale but learns not to react defensively. She has discovered, "it is more important to answer than retreat." (167) Slowly she starts to feel alive again—as though awakening from a long mourning period. As she tries on some of her mother's clothes, little steps reconnect them. Over spring vacation she goes to the track with her dad. He jogs and she walks, but a reconnection starts there too. A connection with her brother Tom, the most angry and defensive in the family, will take longer.

Through the group, Brendan has been given the opportunity to confront one of his main harassers and to educate the others. There will be more harassers and more ignorance to deal with, but he has grown stronger, connected with others, and lost some of his shame. The friendship between Brendan and Susan, though born out of their shared victimization, becomes a major support and comfort for each of them.

The experiment is a success and the six write a letter in support of continuing Mr. Duffy's after-school counseling group. It has made a difference in their lives—without it some of them would have disappeared.

Activities/Topics for Discussion

- How does each member of Susan's family deal with the loss of her mother?
- Words have different power in Kale's life, Brandon's life, and Susan's life. Explain that difference.
- A target often starts to hate the bully or the tormentor. The target's hate is mirrored hate; it mirrors the hate in the bully. Whose hate is more destructive, the bully's or the target's?
- Susan makes a list of things that she would like to tell her father. Why is it difficult for her to talk with him? Is there someone in your life you do not communicate with very well? What would you tell him/her if you could? What stops you?
- Tracee is described on page 169: "Tracee looks away, shaking her head, folded arms matching her crossed legs." Take that position. What does it feel like? What does that body language project?
- After the petition appears in the boys' locker room, Brendan gets a medical excuse and works in the library. He says on page 82, "I loved her [Ms. Henderson] for taking me on, no questions. I was so fucking ashamed that day, that if someone had said the next wrong thing, I would have disappeared." Ashamed of what? How do you think he would have disappeared?
- Have you ever stopped being someone's friend because that person was the target of a bully? Why?
- Define the word "homophobia." Start with a dictionary definition, and then add examples of behaviors you see in your school. The generally accepted statistic is that ten in every one hundred people are gay, so chances are pretty good that you know someone who is gay. Not knowing who around you is gay, evaluate your public behavior. Have your public words and actions been appropriate?
- What is the difference between acceptance and tolerance?
- Who decides if a person is gay?

Quotes for Reader Response

- I pass table after table of students who want nothing to do with me. I hear a few stifled laughs, several variations of the word fat, and one pitying "just look at her." (2)
- "He wants your body," another says, pushing a skinny blond my way. The blond, cackling, holds up his fingers in the sign of the cross. (11)
- "I'm not brave like you. I can barely take what happens at school. I won't go looking for it afterward." (31)
- Whenever I walk with another fat person, I feel twice as big and four times as self-conscious, as if each of us has a flashing neon arrow over our heads pointing down. (35)
- I remember how you used to yell "Rollover" when I would step onto the bus. . . . I remember some girls who were friendly to me at first stopped because of the way you treated me. They didn't want it to happen to them. (46)
- "What is she dressed for, anyway, the dyke olympics? Maybe if she didn't dress like that, she wouldn't be stinking up the place with her BO." (64)
- "You can't tell by looking if a person is gay." Brendan's voice is quiet but steady. (67)
- Silence is our only way through rough times. (76)
- "I don't know why people don't leave each other alone," Randy says, shifting. "Waste of time, people who go out of their way to be shits." (80)
- "Sophomore year, everyone decided I was gay. I started hearing faggot everywhere I went." (81)
- "Why do people get teased?" (94)
- "An ugly girl walks by," Kale says over her. "You're with your friends, you say something. Everyone laughs. BFD. Come on . . . you've never done that?" (94)
- "We have established that words hurt." (93)
- "All this stuff is so new. When you're fat, you're not supposed to think about guys. Or talk about them."
  "Yeah, and at Wayne High, if you're gay, you better . . . pretend you're not." (103)
- "Brendan said he's a virgin. How can he be gay if he's a virgin?" (116)

- "Why I pick on you?" He glances at me, then looks away. "You're fat, and you're alone most of the time. I can do stuff and no one stops me. It's like that. Okay?" (137)
- "I thought it didn't matter. I thought I didn't care." Amber shrugs. "They pulled a train on me, Tracee. Do you know what that means?" (149)
- "I thought I had it bad at this school. It's nothing compared with what Brendan has to go through. I've heard more disgusting, obscene things walking around with him than I have in my whole life." (167)
- "Guys are looking to make each other laugh. Fags are tailor-made for it." (168)
- "Try to give the same kind of understanding you want to receive." (174)
- Brendan says, "You tell me. What was I supposed to do?"
  "You were supposed to quit school," Kale says, glancing at Brendan, past me. "How you held out so long, I don't know." (193)
- "Die, faggot, die." (194)
- I might have disappeared without this class. (198)

Alyssa Brugman, *Walking Naked.*

Set in Australia, *Walking Naked*, realistically portrays the indirect bullying so commonly exhibited by girls everywhere. Megan Twu and Candace Perkins are the founders and unofficial leaders of the most elite group of the eleventh-year females. Their rules, operating procedures, consequences, and devotion to individual members and to the group as a whole keep the group tightly structured. Jessica Chou scouts for new members. Once the group has reviewed Jessica's report, the potential new member receives a trial membership. Later the group discusses and votes on that member. Anyone in the group who strays too far from the guidelines or who participates in behavior unbecoming to the group must go through an intervention. Steps are then taken to correct the problem. Previous interventions have resolved Candace's poor grades, Dara's flirting with a boy already claimed by a group member, Ashley's shoplifting, and Jessica's hairstyle. The group's reputation labels them intelligent, socially involved, fashion conscious, selective, shallow, and cruel when it serves their purpose. Enter Perdita Wiguiggan, the outcast of the whole school. She draws whispered chants of "Freak, Freak, Freak" from Megan and her friends as she passes by in the hallways.

Megan and Perdita are assigned to detention during the same week, and the beginning of an odd friendship forms. Early on, Megan establishes the boundaries—Perdita is not to acknowledge Megan at school and should not expect Megan to acknowledge her in any way. Perdita should look at it as though they play for different teams. The fact that they talk to each other must remain a secret. Slowly the two settle into this restricted relationship based on poetry and each girl's need for a genuine friend.

Of course the group finds out, and though Megan is starting to question her membership in the group, she is about two steps behind where she needs to be. The intervention results in Megan choosing the group's thinking over her own. She rejects Perdita during a particularly needy time, and shortly after, Perdita ends her life. Traumatized by guilt, Megan shuts down. Eventually she resigns from the group and becomes an independent person. In memory of Perdita, Megan starts a poetry group.

Topics for Discussion/Writing

- List the group's rules
- How does the group recruit new members? What values are followed?
- Characterize each group member.
- Make a list of all the words used by the group to describe Perdita.
- Who is the biggest manipulator in the book? What confirms this?
- Explain the purpose of the intervention process.
- How does Perdita survive at school and at home?
- Who in this book are you most like?
- Who in this book would you choose for a friend? Why?
- Explain the importance of group membership.

Quotes for Reader Response

- Every school has one. They are ugly or fat. They have scars or acne or birthmarks. Or maybe it's just something about them that doesn't fit our cherry-lipgloss, video-hits view of how teenagers should be?

  We are mean to them. We call them names. We ridicule them. We make monsters of them. We don't want to stand near them or sit next to them. They repulse us. (3)

- I didn't want to be in the same space as Perdita. I felt a need to get as far away from her as I could. I didn't want to breathe the same air, or smell her. As she approached, I held my breath. (13)

- "It is entirely appropriate that miscreants like myself, those who cannot, or will not, sing the song, those flawed by thoughts conflicting with the spirit of the school, should not be allowed to participate in the school community.

  "We have the power to harm." (15)

- Due to a strong academic record and a prior liaison with Paul Welwood, Katie Gattrell earned herself a trial membership. (21)

- I was sure she didn't take it personally when we called her "the Freak." That was just who she was. It was just something that we did—a bit like "Would you like fries with that?"—after a while it was automatic and you didn't even notice. (24)

- I smiled at her to let her know that it was OK and that she could speak to me. (25)

- What was her problem? She could have at least acknowledged my effort to be nice—especially considering *who I was*. (50)

- The group moved in twos or threes. Nobody went anywhere on their own, ever, not even to the toilet. Being alone suggested "no friends", and despite overwhelming evidence that we were indeed very popular, we couldn't at any point in time allow even the remotest possibility of someone thinking that we were friendless. (73)

- So as we were walking I explained to Perdita that I couldn't see her at school. It wasn't that I didn't like her, I did, for sure. It was just that my position in the group made it impossible. (77)

- "Have you ever felt you were completely alone in the world?" (81)

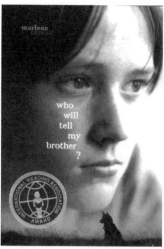

Marlene Carvell, *Who Will Tell My Brother?*

Evan Hill, whose family is Mohawk Indian, has started the quest for self-definition. It begins with his college application, when he decides what to check in the box that asks for ethnic background. He has not felt close to his extended family before, but as that situation changes, he feels more discomfort with the school's Indian caricature mascot. As his brother Jacob has tried before him, Evan follows the proper channels to try to persuade the school board to re-consider the mascot's identity. At first the school board is receptive to Evan's concern, but they cannot see the disrespect. After Evan's fourth visit to the board, they have lost their patience and decide to strengthen their position with a formal proclamation that the mascot will stay. Such is their right.

At school, Evan, quiet, patient, and thoughtful, becomes the target of harassment. The name-calling starts with "Injun" and "Tonto" but quickly proceeds to "timber nigger." Eventually physical violence begins, ranging from threats made at school to the killing of Evan's family dog. As the cruelty becomes known, other students who also feel the disrespect choose to walk with Evan, and he is less alone.

In this novel in verse, the use of language brings an impressive level of solemnity and respect to the story that is missing in the school where it is set. Across America there are sports teams with similar mascots being clung to mostly by white athletes and fans. They do not see the element of disrespect. Harassment is usually judged by the effect on the target. Is there enough evidence that the people these mascots symbolize feel disrespected? This book will lead to lively and emotional discussions.

Activities/Topics for Discussion

- Can you think of other heritages that have been openly mimicked? List as many as possible. List the games you have played as children, the images on TV and in movies, and in history books that mimic other cultures.

- Evan wants to discover his place with his Mohawk family. Why is that so important? Find lines in the book that document his search.
- Evan's older brother Jacob had tried to get the mascot changed and did not succeed. Why does Evan now feel the need to continue this task?
- "My brother did not fail, he only started what has not been finished." (33) It takes a long time to right a wrong. Look at history: How many wrongs are we still trying to correct?
- "But, Evan, racism is a matter of opinion." (72) Who should judge?

Quotes for Reader Response

- We are going to the reservation
  tomorrow
  and I feel the excitement
  building in my brain—
  searching . . . always searching for my place. (7)
- Silas McAllister stumbles
  side to side in mock Indian dancing,
  weaving in and out of prancing girls,
  cardboard cutout hatchet
  raised high above his head. (14)
- "Hey, Evan, if you're an Injun,
  how come you don't look like one?" (22)
- "What does an Injun look like, Martin?
  "You know, black hair in braids,
  red skin; you know, stuff like that." (23)
- I wonder why the color of our
  skin and eyes and hair,
  why the shape of a forehead—
  or nose or chest—
  should determine who we are,
  should determine what we are. (24)
- And so I begin my plea,
  a request for honor,
  for dignity,
  a request to remove an injustice. (37)
- Erasing a picture is easy;
  Erasing an attitude is not. (38)

- They stare at me through the cold, hard eye
  of those who feel threatened,
  whose pride
  whose tradition
  whose bigotry
  and narrow thought
  is threatened. (73)
- And so, the war whoops—
  the underbreath, subtle war whoops
  that follow me through the halls
  must be signs of respect.
  And so I am respected, but the respect
  is shown in fear and hate and cruelty. (85)
- Ignorance and intolerance are passed on
  from one generation to another. (94)
- "Hey, Evan," Silas calls,
  "I hear Injuns eat dog meat;
  did you eat yours?" (129)
- To be indifferent is to promote,
  perhaps even accept, the hate. (132)
- We have done our part
  to show the world
  that hate and shameful pride
  must cease to be. (147)

Jan Cheripko,
Rat.

Fifteen-year-old Jeremy has to testify in court against the school's basketball coach. As the team's manager, Jeremy walked into the coach's office to get a basketball and saw Coach Stennard pinning the head cheerleader, Cassandra Diaz, against the wall, pawing her body, and trying to kiss her. While the coach threatens him, Cassandra has time to escape. Jeremy knows what he has seen is wrong and he tells his parents. Even knowing every member of the basketball team would hate him,

Jeremy testifies against the coach, who is found guilty of attempted rape, assault, battery, unlawful imprisonment, and endangering the welfare of a minor. Coach Stennard goes to jail, and Jeremy returns to school to face the guys on the team. They do not like losing the coach that has taken them to the district championship, so they blame Jeremy. The first day back, the team watches as Jeremy finds a dead rat hanging on his locker.

Simpson is the worst. He had wanted Jeremy to lie and had called Cassandra a slut. After all, the other players would claim she "screwed the basketball team all the time." The whole team stands with Simpson and even supports his verbal harassment as well as Simpson's physical harassment. Jeremy was born with a deformed arm, and when the stares and comments get to be too much, he focuses on shooting baskets. Deep in his concentration Jeremy steps up, jumps, and from out of nowhere a basketball hits him and he crumbles to the floor, landing on his withered arm. As he fights back tears, the rest of the team and former friends point at him and laugh. No one offers help.

Jeremy's father, Dr. Chandler, is also president of the school board, and before he announces the new coach he says, "What's done is done. We have to look ahead to the future." (41) The new basketball coach, Mr. O'Connor, the science teacher, has a different view of things. He believes what Stennard did was wrong and should not be forgotten; he violated a trust and got what he deserved. Coach O'Connor warns, "any one of you who thinks for a moment that he got a raw deal doesn't deserve to belong on my team." (44)

This coach has principles for life and for basketball and demands honesty and effort from his team. He also asks Jeremy to return as team manager. At first the players resent the new coach, but when O'Connor proves his knowledge of basketball strategy and his skill on the court, they start to develop into a team with potential, except for Simpson, who is still angry.

At home, the coach, his wife, and young daughter, Megan, are awaiting the birth of another child; however, Mrs. O'Connor has cancer and there are serious complications. Dr. Chandler, Jeremy's father, becomes involved professionally. Jeremy helps at the O'Connor home, playing with little Megan. Mrs. O'Connor, a kind, sensitive person, helps Jeremy discover some of his potential.

Cheripko fills this book with accessible and valuable lessons about life, basketball, honesty, forgiveness, self-awareness, judgments, and winning. As Coach O'Connor says and Jeremy learns, "It means everything and it means nothing."

Activities/Topics for Discussion/Writing

- Why did Coach O'Connor choose Jeremy to be team manager?
- How do bullies know a victim's vulnerable spot? Who knows Jeremy's?
- Jeremy is harassed for two reasons: because he has a withered arm and because he testified against Coach Stennard. Explain why he is bullied for each of these.
- If you were on the basketball team, how would you treat Jeremy? Simpson? Cassandra?
- There are three families discussed in this book: the Chandlers, the O'Connors, and Simpson Theodore and his parents. Compare and contrast the three.
- Simpson has a difficult time growing up, which may explain the way he treats people. When are his actions his responsibility? When should he be held accountable for his actions?
- Though Cassandra and Jeremy did nothing wrong, they are both punished by others. Why do you think people treated them so badly?
- Break the class into groups and divide the Twelve Principals of Concept Basketball among the groups. Ask each group to explain the one assigned to them with examples from life.

Quotes for Reader Response

- I wanted to laugh to be brave, but I knew if I made a sound, I'd cry—or worse, puke. So I just turned and walked to homeroom, listening to them chant, "Buzza Rat! Buzza Rat! Buzza Rat!" (20)
- I lost myself in a make-believe world I know how to create whenever I want to. I've been doing that for years. Ever since I was a little kid and other kids started to make fun of my withered stump of an arm. (24)
- Now I can tell you, you never been alone in life until you're lyin' in the middle of a gym with kids laughin' at you and starin' at you, and not one of them will come over to ask you if you're all right. (36)
- I always saw them as my friends. But it was weird, when all this happened, it was like they all grouped together—against me. (42)
- Honesty is the First Principle of everything. (55)

- "I'm tired of telling the truth. It doesn't do any good. I told the truth once, and all it did was cause trouble. I don't have any friends." (87)
- I can do lots of things, even though I got a bad arm, but sometimes I feel like Dad doesn't think I'm quite complete. That, somehow, because of my arm, I'm gonna be some kinda freak or invalid all my life. (114)
- "You antagonize, tease, and harass Jeremy, but he's the only one here who has the guts to tell the truth, no matter what it costs him." (122)
- "You're all rats, just like the little weasel with the scrawny arm." Then Simpson looks right at me. "Your old man shoulda made you an abortion when he had the chance." (124)
- "So I've been good about my arm, God. But why is it you're letting Simpson loose on me? What did I do to deserve that' And why do I have to be all alone, anyway, God? That I don't understand. And I wonder, God, since we're talking, why did you have me born?" (130)
- "Jeremy, maybe you don't know this about yourself, but you have one of the greatest gifts of all—you have a conscience. Telling the truth is important to you." (150)
- I think I'm tired of growing up. (153)

Chris Crutcher, *Whale Talk.*

T. J. Jones, an adopted child with a multicultural heritage (black, white, Japanese), has fought his way through abandonment by his mother and the rage that followed. He is made up of tightly woven moral fiber that does not allow him to stand by while someone is abused. When Chris Coughlin wears his dead brother's varsity jacket, senior football player Mike Barbour goes ballistic on him with insults. Chris suffered brain damage from abusive acts when he was a child; his older brother was his hero, and the jacket is all he has left of him. T. J.

steps in and takes on the conflict as a mission. It isn't until Mr. Simet, journalism/English teacher, wants T. J.'s help to start a swim team, using the only swimming pool available at All Night Fitness which measures a short twenty yards, that T. J. sees a way for Chris to earn a letter jacket of his own.

Eventually, T. J. assembles a team: Chris Coughlin, the brain damaged kid, now too frightened to wear his brother's varsity jacket; Daniel Hole, a brilliant guy who only talks in mega-syllabled words; Tay-Roy Kibble, a musically gifted and intensely focused body-builder; Simon DeLong, weighing in at 300 plus, and as wide as he is tall; Jackie Craig, a ghost of a boy, who has never mumbled an audible word; and Andy Mott, an edgy, sarcastic mass-murder type who has one bionic leg. A team of out-casts. A team of individuals who are the usual targets for the football team and its groupies, the former players and hangers-on whose lives peaked on the high school football field and who have never moved on. Rick Marshall leads this highly visible and influential group referred to as the Wolverines Too.

There are many levels of bullying and harassment in this book. Mike Barbour and Rich Marshall are racist, harassing not just T. J. but anyone of color, including Rich's stepdaughter. Both are abusive to women, physically, emotionally, and mentally. Rich is worse, but he is training Mike. These two, most of the football team, the male coaches, and the principal hold earning the varsity jacket up there with earning the Congressional Metal of Honor, and the swim team boys certainly do not deserve even a chance at such glory.

The swim team guys just keep working. They have never had a chance to belong to anything before, and they do not want to mess up. Their workouts give them a shared space and a sense of community that grows during their long road trips to swim meets. First with hints, then small risks, and finally a trusting openness, they become a tighter unit than T. J. ever dreamed could happen, and he never wants to let them down. With Coach Semet's help, they come up with a plan that should assure varsity jackets for every member.

Crutcher shows us not only the fears and histories of these swim kids, but also the fears and histories of guys like Mike Barbour and Rich Marshall. Everyone has a story, and no one is free of scars. Some of these guys will heal: some won't. Wisdoms and realities hit like bombs throughout this book. Be prepared with referral resources and stay sensitive to what your students don't say. Give them opportunities for private venting, processing through vehicles like dialogue journals, response journals, or private conference time.

Don't ever expect to look at an athlete as a simple stereotype again.

Activities/Topics for Discussion/Writing

- The athletes in this school are considered heroes. Why? Why not the kids who do community service? Or get high grades? Or have the most friends?
- Why is T. J. such a strong advocate for Chris Coughlin?
- Oliver Van Zandt, a.k.a. Icko, works two fast-food jobs and secretly lives in the health club, sleeping under benches, all so he can send his son to college. What sacrifices have been made for you? What sacrifices have you made for someone else?
- T. J.'s father unknowingly killed a child. That event became the defining moment in his life. How can one moment define a life?
- Rich Marshall has trouble moving beyond high school, which seems to be a power base for him. What clues does this give about his life?
- What racial influences exist in northern Idaho and eastern Washington of the USA? What hate groups have moved there? Go to www.tolerance.org/maps/hate/index.html on the Internet. What hate groups exist in your area?
- How has Rich's racism affected Heidi? Rich is Heidi's stepfather. How has it affected Alicia, Rich's wife and Heidi's mother? How has it affected Rich? What has that racism cost him?

Quotes for Reader Response

- So my mind tells me all racists are either ignorant or so down on themselves they need somebody to be better than. (3)
- You get treated like shit, then have to be ashamed that you're the kind of person people treat like shit. (18)
- When I see someone getting kicked I feel it. (42)
- I love the way life can put things in perspective for you. (45)
- It's a lot easier to hear that word [nigger] than to say it to a little kid, because I know the impact when you aren't steeled against it. (68)
- She looks sadly into my eyes. "You're a dirty nigger, too." (69)
- Despair moves in like a flash flood when she is degraded. (71)
- A group of real outsiders, a group Cutter High school has offered very little to. (88)

- "This is the first time in eleven years anyone has paid one bit of attention to him [Chris], other than to make him drink urine out of a Seven-Up can or trick him into giving a dog an erection." (93)
- "They'll think a one-legged asshole is a lot funnier than a fat guy." (100)
- When rage takes you over, you do what the rage tells you. (146)
- "The Mike Barbours and Rich Marshalls of the world have just as much right to exist as you do." (149)
- "I don't know what I'm going to do when this is over. I never belonged to . . . anything. I was never on a team, never chosen . . ." (184)
- Nothing exists without its opposite. (204)
- "Not one minute for revenge." (212)

Sharon M. Draper, *The Battle of Jericho.*

The Warriors of Distinction have been around for fifty years. Several former members of this community service organization have become leaders in the community. Every year seniors and selected juniors take a decorated Christmas tree to the local orphanage, and collect, sort, and deliver gifts to needy families for Christmas, Hanukkah, and Kwanzaa. The Warriors of Distinction started as a school club, but over the years the group has become more independent and now maintains only a loose connection with the high school through an informal advisor. Rumors about the pledge week and the oath of silence have drawn suspicions.

Jericho Prescott and his cousin, Josh Prescott, are more like brothers than cousins. Raised by their parents in apartments next to each other, they have gone through seventeen years together. The Warriors of Distinction have approached both young men, and the excitement of wearing their own Warrior jacket, of being part of this very influential and respected organization, makes their heads spin. It all seems too good to be true.

After the celebratory New Year's Eve party, Jericho, Josh, friends Kofi and Dana, the first female to force her way into the group, excitedly join eleven other juniors in what turns out to be their worst nightmare. During Pledge Week, the last week of January, "Pledge Slime" must follow all orders given by the seniors and keep their vow of silence. Each morning at school, the juniors receive their orders for the day, which usually involve service to the school community and maintaining the Warriors' public image. Each night, in an old warehouse, the "Bonding of Brotherhood" takes place. Each must promise to up-hold these basic guidelines:

- A Warrior of Distinction is not afraid to lower himself for his brother.
- A Warrior of Distinction does not show fear.
- A Warrior of Distinction is bonded to his brothers.
- A Warrior of Distinction never breaks the code of silence.
- A Warrior of Distinction celebrates obedience. (70–71)

The first night the pledges are blindfolded. The senior members have spit into a bowl. The pledges are told they must swallow a spoonful from the bowl, which really only contains raw egg whites. After removing their blindfolds, they are made to run, circling the warehouse until they are told to stop. Senior Eddie Mahoney makes sure no one slows down. If anyone does, Eddie hits the slacker with the handle of a snow shovel. Thirty minutes later, they are told to stop, circle up, and remove their shirts. Dana, the only female, is the last to remove hers. She stands quietly, half-naked, staring straight ahead. Slowly the other pledges silently surround her, facing outward. Each pledge receives a pink t-shirt with the slogan, "I am not distinguished yet" to wear the rest of the week.

Dog collars, severe paddlings, and urine-filled toilet swirlies intensify the hazing each night. Senior Eddie harasses Dana openly and no one stops him. The code of silence rules their lives and eventually takes one. On the last night, after being force-fed whisky and led into a condemned house near the old warehouse, each pledge must take the "Leap of Faith." Fifty years earlier that meant to jump off a chair while blindfolded. These pledges have to jump, still partly drunk, out of a second-story window into a stack of padding covered with mud. Eddie stands behind them with a gun as they each slowly take the leap. Most are not harmed, but Josh, the last one to jump, tragically hits his head on a rock and dies.

At what point did the initiation change to hazing? The degradation, the humiliation, the fear, the threats, the gun, and the danger were all protected by the code of silence and the pledge, "All of us or none of us." No one would betray their word, and so they betrayed a life. What would a young person do to fit in? What won't a young person do to fit in?

Activities/Topics for Discussion

- How do the Warriors have everyone fooled?
- Why is the code of silence needed?
- Eric Bell lives in a wheelchair. He explains to Jericho how his spine was injured. On a hot August day, Eric and some buddies were playing Daredevil in the park near Hartwell pool. They came up with a dare to climb the fence and jump into the water. Eric heard his back snap as he landed. What does this scene foreshadow?
- Eric is an engaging young man. How is he treated by many of the student population?
- On page 105, Jericho has just received a car for Christmas. "Can we trust you, Jericho?" his father asked finally. "I will never make you sorry, Dad. Promise." Does Jericho keep his promise? Why is his promise to his father not as strong as his promise to the Warriors?
- There are many examples of foreshadowing in the book. Make a list of as many as you can find.
- Who is more reckless, Josh or Jericho? Explain your answer.
- What is your definition of a person of distinction? Who in the book fits your definition? Who in your life?
- Explain Arielle's behavior at the end of the book. Why do you think she broke up with Jericho?
- Jericho felt uncomfortable and believed that the pledging had crossed the line. Why didn't he do anything?
- What were the pledges willing to do to fit in? What are you willing to do to fit in? What do you do every day to fit in? What is the worst thing you have ever done to be part of the "in crowd"?

- Anytime you are asked to swear to secrecy, ask yourself why. A person who has nothing to hide has no secrets. Do you agree?

Quotes for Reader Response

- "Not one word of what we say or do from this point on is to be shared with another living soul—not your mother, your father, your girlfriend, your priest, not even your shadow on the sidewalk." (67)
- Madison continues "We ask for, no—we demand—your dedication, your absolute obedience, your very life, if necessary." (68)
- "The Bonding of the Brotherhood," Madison explained, "requires not only secrecy and obedience, but also responsibility, loyalty, and honor." (68)
- Jericho did not like the sound of this, but he wasn't sure how to get out of it. He whispered the words. His stomach was starting to hurt. (69)
- "Sometimes the Lord takes care of the stupid; sometimes the stupid gotta think for themselves." (88)
- "After you make the team, the returning players put the new kids through hazing rituals." (150)
- "I didn't want to be a part of the hazing, but I didn't have guts enough to stop it." (151)
- "And we will call each of you by your proper title, which is 'Pledge Slime.'" (154)
- "Did you know hazing is illegal in forty-one states?" Mr. Boston asked. (184)
- Somehow he couldn't quite remember why he'd wanted so badly to be a member of the Warriors of Distinction. (205)
- "I just gotta be in this club. I'll be nobody at school if I fail the pledging process—less than nobody." (213)
- "You will jump from the window a lowly piece of Pledge Slime, but you will arise, like a phoenix, as a respected and honored member of the Warriors of Distinction!" (252)
- Eddie pulled a gun from his jacket. "I asked," he repeated ominously as he pointed the gun at each of them, "who will be first?" (253)
- "He [Josh] would have said that there's nothing very distinguished about death." (295)

Alex Flinn, *Breaking Point.*

Paul Richmond wants to belong; however, circumstances beyond his control have made him a loner. Because his dad was in the military, his family of three moved nearly every year. Paul's mother decided to home-school Paul to protect him from all the changes. From second grade to ninth, Paul and his mother were a unit while his father worked late, left home early. Then Lt. Colonel Richmond decided the marriage wasn't working and he left for good. Paul and his mom later learned the lieutenant colonel's secretary was pregnant. After the divorce, in order to make money and to ensure Paul a good education, Laura Richmond takes an office job at Gate-Brickell Christian, the most expensive private school in Miami.

Using Gate-Brickell as a setting allows Flinn to describe the elite, wealthy student culture. They have the adults on campus convinced that they are the respectable, worthy leaders of the school. Because they seem to have it all and are envied by everyone, they find other ways to amuse themselves. These students also make life miserable for the other students, most of whom will take any abuse to fit in. But the sons and daughters of the exceedingly rich don't have time for charity cases. Charlie Good is an exception. He often takes poor classmates under his wing—if he can use them. Charlie slowly lures Paul, who is willing to do nearly anything to belong to Charlie's crowd.

David Blanco is the usual target. His father is the school's custo-dian, and his mother is the cook. Besides being working-class, David sports many tattoos and body piercings along with bleached white hair. Charlie and his two thugs, Meat and St. John, harass David and his par-ents. As a warning, David's dog is killed, its body posted in front of the school, and the head left on the family doorstep. The year before, Charlie had favored David the same way he starts favoring Paul.

Feeling honored to be included, Paul joins Charlie, Meat, and St. John on a late-night mailbox-smashing raid, which not only entangles Paul but also reveals his deep anger as he uses a baseball bat to beat a mailbox into a twisted metal lump. At school Charlie ignores Paul until his loyalty is proven when Paul, a computer wiz, hacks into the school data bank and changes Charlie's D in biology. Now he even gets to eat lunch with the in-crowd.

As the story continues, the stunts become more serious. Pressure on David soars, and he sees no way out except by suicide. Paul is there when David jumps from the tower. Two senior athletes have raced to get help while Paul tries to calm David. The principal rushes to the tower to fix things instead of calling the police. Appearances must be protected. The day after David dies, it is business as usual at school—but not for Paul. In his anger and frustration at the school, he agrees to Charlie's latest request, to plant a bomb in the ceiling of the biology teacher's classroom.

The story is told in flashbacks. In the prologue, Paul, on his eighteenth birthday, has just been released from two years in juvenile detention. Chapter 1 starts with his first day at Gate-Brickell as a sophomore.

Topics for Discussion/Writing

- Paul is an only child; Charlie is an only child. How are their families alike? How are they different?
- List the people in the book who are bullies. What behaviors define them as bullies?
- List the people in the book who are victims/targets. What made each of them targets?
- Most of the people in the book are witnesses to bullying. How did they respond? How would you have responded?
- What is the significance of the Sermons? How do their titles relate to the events that are happening when a particular sermon is delivered?

> Love Thine Enemies
> Whatsoever Ye Do Unto the Least of My Brothers, Ye Do
>   Unto Me
> Thou Shalt Not Steal
> How the Holy Spirit Convicts Abusers of Power
> The Terror of Temptations

- What is Binky's role in the story?
- How does Charlie manipulate others?
- How is power an aphrodisiac for Charlie? For Paul?
- Why did Charlie's mother help Paul? What was her motivation?

Quotes for Reader Response

- "Any sign of weakness, they eat you alive." (3)
- "We don't take well to newcomers unless you're someone important. Are you?" (3)
- *Please let me make more friends. Please let me be popular.* I was ashamed of the wish. (39)
- Meat and St. John emerged from the truck, laughing, slapping me on the back, and whatever I'd felt disappeared. For the first time since coming to Miami—the first time ever, maybe—I belonged. Everything had changed. (65)
- It had been almost two weeks since Charlie had initiated me into the Mailbox Club. He still ignored me at school. (72)
- I knew that with Charlie, I was safe. Charlie could get away with anything. (83)
- With his hand, he beckoned me over. I didn't want to go. Yet it was like he had a remote control. (97)
- It was then I faced my mistake. I'd offended Charlie. That wasn't something you did. But I wasn't mad at Charlie. I was mad at myself for not appreciating what I had. (103)
- I was still dazed, wondering where it had come from. That anger. That violence in me. And then, the high, better than alcohol, the high of having hurt someone else for once, instead of the other way around. (137)

Ron Koertge, *The Brimstone Journals.*

Done in free verse, this book offers a nice alternative and can bridge into the many teen books written in this format. Each page presents the thoughts of a student at Brimstone High School. Fifteen kids tell the story of a high school nurturing a crisis.

Lester dramatically opens the book as he is holding his dad's gun and imagining who he would get even with at school for all the tormenting he has endured. Overweight, good-hearted, but slower intellectually than the other kids, Lester is an easy target, and more than any other character, he touches the reader. Lester, recruited into the Brotherhood by Boyd, shows how far a kid will go to fit in somewhere. The son of an alcoholic, Boyd, whose only code is "Break all rules," is on his way to becoming a "rage-aholic." Meredith, eighteen and legal, likes sex and older guys; she befriends Lester and saves him from making the mistake of helping the Brotherhood blow up the school. Tran, a second-generation Vietnamese, quietly observes the craziness of Brimstone. Sheila thinks she may be a lesbian. Damon, the stereotypical jock, not only harasses Lester but he also keeps his girlfriend, Kelli, on a short leash by making her carry a pager and a cell phone. Kelli is trying to break away. Neesha rejects standard English because it is the "white man sway." Joseph has "save-the-earth" hippie parents; he feels guilty if he throws out a pop can. Allison's stepfather likes to give her backrubs while she tries to do her homework. Jennifer's family is right-wing Christian and she wants to experience some fun. Carter, black, rich, and classy, doesn't fit in anywhere. Kitty wants to be so thin she could fly.

Just like in every other high school, students with different backgrounds, cultures, abilities, and interests fill the hallways. But at Brimstone, someone has made a hit list of people to get even with!

Topics for Discussion/Writing

- How many different types of harassment can be found in this book? List them.
- List every character that harasses/bullies someone.
- List every character that is harassed/bullied by someone.
- Compare these two lists. Discuss why some characters show up on both lists.
- What will kids do to fit in? Cite examples from the book and in your school.
- List the characters who do try to fit in.
- What would most teachers think of Damon? Lester? Jennifer? Neesha? Others?
- Explain how the book presentation (verse form, fifteen first-person narratives), could develop empathy in the reader. Define empathy using examples from the book.
- Which character are you most like? Least like?
- Who would you want for a friend? For what reasons?
- Who would you not want for a friend? For what reasons?

- What is the difference between Boyd and Lester that Lester goes to the police for help?
- Who is on Boyd's list?
- How is this high school different from other high schools, especially yours?

Quotes for Reader Response

- Ms. Malone says black
  people have their own Heaven, but it's
  far enough away from ours so we won't
  have to listen to their music. (29)
- I'm about half-sick to my stomach all
  the time because I'm scared.
  Those jocks come down the hall like
  a tidal wave of muscle. On a good day
  they only knock me into the wall once. (36)
- I'm like 5'4" and I want
  to pee mine [pants] just about every day walking
  into high school. I saw Damon come down
  so hard on Lester the other day I couldn't
  believe it. (57)
- I'm nothing now but a fat kid. (58)
- Mike and I welcomed Lester to the Brotherhood.
  We beat on him pretty good, and he took it.
  Now we're bonded. (59)
- So I'm in.
  And I've got a split lip to show for it. (63)
- This morning Meredith said she liked
  my new look.
  When's the last time a girl talked to me first? (63)
- I told Jennifer what she wanted
  to hear.
  It was so easy I'm kind of ashamed
  to get double points for [doing] her. (74)
- You know what nonviolent means: *nothing
  ever changes.* (79)

Aisha Muharrar, *More than a Label: Why What You Wear or Who You're with Doesn't Define Who You Are.* Nonfiction.

Aisha Muharra, was only fourteen when Columbine happened, and like so many young people in our country, the event deeply affected her. She needed to do something. The news from Columbine drew attention to the many ways teens judge each other. Labels—old ones like "jock," which has crossed into everyday use, to unfamiliar ones like "goth," new on the scene and possibly ephemera—were splashed across the media. Working with Free Spirit Publishing, Muharrar created a survey about labels and sent out that survey to teens across the country. More than a thousand kids responded, and Muharrar used many of those voices in creating her book. She was seventeen years old when she finished it.

In my work with schools, I suggest using *More than a Label* and the teen survey as a starting point. The survey (a copy is available in Muharrar's book with permission to photocopy it for classroom use) is well done and provides an excellent back-door approach to the discussion of bullying and harassment. Students willingly complete the anonymous survey because it is about them. In the discussion that follows, I sit back and listen as each group spews out the same observations and wisdoms as other groups I have worked with. Of course, on that first day, none of them admit to calling other people those labels! Slowly they will admit to using them, but only in a kidding way—never seriously. They sound very much like adults.

In chapter 2, Muharrar lists the five factors most likely used to assign labels:

- clothing style/appearance,
- interests/activities/music preferences,
- behavior/personality,
- grades/intellect,
- friends. (27)

Other factors include "wealth or lack of it, race or ethnic background, religion, hometown, being male or female." (27) Some of these last factors were given to us at birth; we couldn't choose them. When I ask students to create a social ladder for their school, appearance is always at the top. No wonder they spend hours trying for the right look.

Labels can do some damage, but the real damage happens when the individual buys into them, and negative self-talk is how we do that. Muharrar points out that when we are mean to ourselves, call ourselves names—no one else is around to defend us. Kids who take other people's cruel words and identify with those words so closely that they use those names on themselves give up any power they had in the situation. It is hard to be your only advocate; that's why friends have to step up. When teens dialogue about this issue, they develop some skills to help them support targets instead of bullies.

In chapter 6, "Slurs and other Hate Words," Muharrar warns readers that there are shocking words in this chapter that will offend some people. She explains her reason for printing them: "I realized that if teens hear hate speech every day, I *have* to write about it." (91) She had intended to only write about labels, but because the surveys showed many teens were labeled with these hate words, Muharrar discusses these words openly and says the issue needs to be addressed. Slurs are much worst than labels: they not only hurt, they can make a person hate. The target's hate mirrors the perpetrator's hate.

This book is an easy sell to students for several reasons. Most important it is nonfiction and the author is one of them. When they read something in *More than a Label* and identify with it, they are identifying with another human being. And if these other teens are saying and feeling these things, then it must be okay for the reader to feel them too.

Activities/Topics for Discussion

This book contains many practical and effective activities. Below are a few of my own or my favorites from the book.

- Create a list of all the labels heard in your school.
- Draw a huge ladder on the board or on newsprint. Add the labels from your list to the ladder to create a social ladder for your school. This could also be a bulletin board activity.
- Write a letter to the person you are from the person you want to be.
- If you have ever been called a label, make a list of all the things about you that do not fit that label.

- What special factors might exist in your school that separates kids into categories? (One elementary school had problems between kids who rode the bus and kids who walked to school.)
- How do popular kids bully others?
- Discuss the difference between labels that attack girls' sexuality and labels that attack boys' sexuality.
- To find out if you are a bully, answer the questions on page 107.
- Create a personal contract in which you agree to do something about labeling in your everyday life. Write it down and seal it in an envelope addressed to you. Ask a trusted friend to hold it for one month and then mail it to you.

Quotes for Reader Response

- Labels that people gave each other—or themselves—were like invisible nametags. Once you started to "wear" one, everyone was free to make assumptions about who you are. (13)
- A huge number of teens have been the victims of slurs—or words that attack your race, religion, gender, or sexual orientation. (17)
- According to the Teen Labels Survey, 86 percent of teens said they had been labeled. (18)
- Consider the fact that a person is so much more than a label. (21)
- "I don't know why we are so mean to the nerds or the other teens who don't hang out with us. I guess I do it because everybody else does it. I wish I could stop, but I still want to stay popular. It's the thing I thrive on." (50)
- Many teens talked about how they like their labels and actually chose them for themselves. (51)
- "I never want to be popular. Most popular kids at my school are mean to kids who aren't popular; and it makes kids feel so bad." (54)
- Labeling is actually a type of peer pressure. When you label, you assign someone an identity—you tell that person who he is or should be. (55)
- Label Radar is a personal screening process that helps us decide what types of people we'll befriend. (61) ·
- "Hate speech generally does what it's intended to do—it makes you feel hated."(93)
- School violence may be the final step in a series of actions that spiral out of control. Slurs play a role here. (104)

- Sometimes, living with a label can lead you to lose track of who you are. (113)
- Focus on your life—not on other people's lives. (117)
- If you address people by their actual names instead of labels, you'll be sending a message to others that you don't use labels anymore. (121)

Carol Plum-Ucci, *What Happened to Lani Garver?*

Hackett Island does not take well to strangers; summer tourists from Philadelphia are tolerated for the cash they bring in, but the fishermen rule the home turf. The bullying in this book is rooted in homophobia and grows to gay bashing. Some island kids start a slur campaign that influences some and endangers others. No one in this book discloses that he is gay, but the perception of someone being gay leads to the destruction of many lives. This book is about perceptions, not realities.

Lani (pronounced Lonny) Garver arrives. Lani is tall, slim, with shoulder-length hair, a baby-blush complexion, and delicate features. Is this person a boy or a girl? Lani answers the question with, "I am not a girl!" That is not good enough. Claire McKenzie, the narrator and a young woman with her own baggage, tells us in the prologue that the Fish Frat drowned Lani. He had only been on Hackett Island for five days.

On Wednesday, Claire meets Lani at school and is the only one on Hackett who connects with him. Their friendship is sudden, honest, and lifesaving for Claire. Life has not been easy for Lani, and his experiences have earned him a wisdom and understanding resembling that of an aged elder. Through gentle questions, Lani pulls out Claire's history. She is a leukemia survivor, having spent most of her middle-school years in treatment in Philadelphia. Her friends never talk about it. Claire's mother copes by drinking; her father and his new wife live in

Philadelphia, and that is where Claire lived while undergoing chemo. Since her return to Hackett, she has developed an eating disorder and is afraid the leukemia has recurred. She takes care of her mother, doesn't want to trespass into her father's new life, allows her best friend Macy to make all her decisions, and doesn't allow herself to feel any anger. Because she won't deal with that emotion—it deals with her. Lani tells Claire that she has "issues" and convinces her to be tested at a free clinic in the city to see if the leukemia has returned.

On their trip to the clinic, their friendship takes on magical qualities as the topic of floating angels keeps coming up. Claire begins to wonder if Lani is a floating angel; some people she meets that day believe it to be true.

Back at Coast Regional High School, not everyone values Lani. Trouble is kindled by misinterpretations that soon are accepted realities. (The book does a good job of explaining how perceptions quickly become factual evidence, and how people cling to what they think they have seen.) Lani comes on to Tony, or did Tony come on to Lani? Who believes the new he/she kid anyway? Has Claire become a fag-hag and should she be saved from herself? Far too soon, Lani and Claire are fighting for his life.

Topics for Discussion or Writing

- Characterize the "Fish Frat."
- List the homophobic slurs made in the book.
- Explain how the conflicts were already set between the islanders and outsiders.
- What is their treatment of Lani based on?
- Does any factual evidence exist that proves Lani is gay? Explain.
- Does any factual evidence exist that proves Tony is gay? Explain.
- At what point does the gay-bashing begin?
- Define "floating angels." Do they exist? Could they exist? What in this book could persuade someone to believe that Lani Garver was a floating angel?
- What character in this book are you most like? Hope you are like?

Quotes for Reader Response

- "Truth and belief are a stallion and a mule." (xiii)

- "There's a difference between stereotyping and deciding where somebody fits in."
  "What's the difference? It's all for the purpose of passing judgement." (45)
- "Seeing through human behavior is, like, a blessing and a curse." (47)
- "You got to pay your dues to sing the blues." (107)
- My friends would have seen something that hadn't happened, just so life could make sense to them. (204)
- "'Monsterizing.' It's when you erroneously make someone out to be a monster to justify your own behavior toward that person." (240)
- There was nothing to do but admit this was real. (257)
- Message to God: Do something. (258)
- "You almost lost your lives, diving for some goddamn flake in a nightgown! That's what he was, Claire! A whining, whimp-o, fucking weirdo. And nobody is going to jail over him!" (271)

Lois-Ann Yamanaka, *Name Me Nobody.*

Set on the Big Island of Hawaii, the culture in this novel is mainly created through the use of island dialect. Teenagers always seem to have their own language, but these island teens, most of mixed heritage, may seem difficult to understand at first. Emi-Lou Kaya and Yvonne Vierra, each an only child, have practically been raised as sisters. Emi-Lou's grandparents and Yvonne's parents have been best friends and extended family for as long as anyone can remember. Emi-Lou's own mother, Roxanne, was only sixteen when Emi-Lou was born and either wasn't sure of or refused to identify the father. At thirty, Roxanne still doesn't know how to be an adult. Emi-Lou's grandmother and Von are the only real family Emi-Lou has. The girls have watched out for each other since nursery school, and at nine years old, they take a blood oath, swearing that they would always be together. Yvonne, the protector, and Emi-Lou, the supporter, have kept that pledge.

The summer after eighth grade, Von, a natural athlete, wants to join the island's women's softball team, the Hilos Astros, one of the top teams in the league. Uncle Charlie has worked a deal with the coach: Yvonne can play if Emi-Lou plays too. For Louie, playing on that team would be a living nightmare. A shy, timid girl, Louie is harassed by other students because of her weight, and being on that team would make her more available to her harassers. But for Von and her hope of a college scholarship, Louie agrees. Von decides she will be Louie's trainer and help her lose weight and get fit.

At fourteen, Von is the youngest player on the Astros. Von's father worries because lesbians play on the team. Emi-Lou doesn't believe Von is "butchie," but sees that as a possible threat to their friendship. When Von starts spending time with Babes from the team, Louie gets jealous.

The diet, exercise, and pills work, and by the end of the summer, a re-created Emi-Lou starts ninth grade with a new look and a new wardrobe—but the same insides. Though still feeling inadequate, she helps her friend Rudy campaign for student body president, writes several articles for the school newspaper, and gets her first crush on Kyle, the handsome bad-boy in her journalism class. Finally, she is starting to create her own niche at school, much as Von has done with the softball team.

The Hilo Astros win the Big Island Women's Softball League Championship, and Yvonne is chosen for the All-Island First Team Picks, the youngest to receive All-Star honors in the history of the league. But after her name is called, she doesn't turn to Louie, she turns and hugs Babes.

Events start to pile up. After discovering Von and Babes are lovers, Emi-Lou physically attacks Babes at school, Yvonne's parents find out about the relationship, and even though Emi-Lou was not the one who told, Yvonne won't talk to her or look at her.

Homosexuality is a major theme in this book. There are several gay characters—all good people, although some have rough edges—and the lesson learned by the end of the book is acceptance of people as they are, not what we want them to be, with Emi-Lou's grandmother conveying the most wisdom.

Because of the homosexuality, this book probably won't be taught in some school districts, or even be available, though it certainly should be. You know your district and the politics that exist; perhaps this book can be presented as an individual reading option.

Activities/Topics for Discussion

- There are two groups harassed in this story: overweight people and gay people. You probably hear attacks on these people in your school. Why does it seem acceptable to pick on these people?
- How much does the media influence the public's perception of the perfect body image? How realistic is that image?
- Emi-Lou tells her grandmother that the more she hassles her, the more Emi-Lou wants to stay fat. Have you ever rebelled by doing something that you knew was not in your best interests? Have you ever done something just because your parents/mentor told you not to? Why do you think we behave that way?
- Emi-Lou realizes she used her fat as a defense in the world, a type of insulation. We all need defenses in life, but some defenses are healthier than others. Make two lists, one of healthy defenses and one of unhealthy defenses. Which ones do you choose the most often?
- There are several homosexual characters in the book. List them and describe their personalities.
- Uncle Charlie and Emi-Lou change the most in their judgment of Yvonne's sexual orientation. What did they believe in the beginning of the book, what did they believe by the end of the book, and what helped them change?
- In what ways is the character of Sterling important in the book?
- In what ways does the island dialect add or detract from the telling of the story?

Quotes for Reader Response

- That's what I am. A nobody bastard girl. (2)
- "Emi-oink," they say as they lift their noses with their index fingers. Their subclique of wanna-bes giggle like a Greek chorus. (7)
- I'm not smart enough to be a nerd. I'm not stink enough to be a turd. I fall somewhere right below the band geeks and right above the zeroes. (7)
- Sometimes the Jap-girls call me Emi-loser. Sometimes they call me Emi-lez. (8)
- In Ivy Nursery School, Von held my hand throughout the day and protected me from the girl bullies who were quick with their hands and words. (9)

- The teachers think we don't know about high, medium, or low sections. But we do. It makes some kids feel like turds, that is, those of us turds not labeled gifted and talented. (18)
- I'm the fat bat-girl. "C'mon grab those bats. I don't want any of my girls hurt because of a good-for-nothing slow ass daydreamer." (24)
- This body Von creates for me through starvation, pep talks, fistfuls of pills, sweat, mind-over-matter, and exercise is not me. All of a sudden, there's nothing between me and the world. (49)
- I look at myself in the mirror. I still feel like me. I still see the same me. How come everybody's seeing somebody else? I was nobody fat. Am I somebody skinny? (52)
- "Go get your bag," Gina whispers in my ear, "you bench-warming lez." (66)
- This according to Von, who thinks my participation in student gov activities is stupid; student gov is full of babies, dorks, the uncool; a waste of time, phony, elitist; a bunch of ass-kissing wanna-bes. (71)
- "And Louie—kinda looking chunky, eh. Ten more pounds and Sterling be too shame to be seen with Emi-fat . . ." (166)
- "For the boys you gotta look right and be seen with the right chicks, and you, Louie, you just ain't right." (209)
- My grandma helps me understand that nothing can ever be how it used to be. "Life ain't that way," she tells me. "You always move on to what's next." (215)
- "You cannot force somebody to be who you want them to be." (216)

Annotated Bibliography

Selected Short Stories

Adler, C. S. "Michael's Little Sister." In *Am I Blue?* Ed. by Marion Dane Bauer. New York: HarperTrophy, 1994. 149–62. Michael's little sister Becky punches a kid at school for calling Michael a fag. She needs to know the truth, and when she does, her acceptance is complete.

Bauer, Joan. "A Letter from the Fringe." In *On the Fringe*. Ed. by Donald R. Gallo. New York: Dial Books, 2001. 181–91. Feeling that she and her friends have been targets for too long, Dana considers writing a letter to the school newspaper about their plight.

———. "The Truth About Sharks." In *From One Experience to Another: Award-Winning Authors Sharing Real-Life Experiences Through Fiction*. Ed. by M. Jerry Weiss and Helen S. Weiss. New York: Forge, 1997. 32–47. When Beth is falsely accused of shoplifting by a bullying security guard, she finds a clever way to rectify the situation.

Carter, Alden R. "Satyagraha." In *On the Fringe*. Ed. by Donald R. Gallo. New York: Dial Books, 2001. 165–77. Harassed by the school's all-conference defensive end, Ramdas Bahave uses his wits to change his nemesis' behavior.

Coville, Bruce. "Am I Blue?" In *Am I Blue?* Ed. by Marion Dane Bauer. New York: HarperTrophy, 1994. 3–16. Fairy godfather Melvin comes to the aid of Vincent, a perceived-to-be-gay young man.

Crutcher, Chris. "A Brief Moment in the Life of Angus Bethune." In *Athletic Shorts: Six Short Stories*. New York: Greenwillow, 1991. 3–25. Because Angus is seriously overweight and has gay parents, he's been the victim of bullies for a long time, until this one special evening.

———. "Fourth and Too Long." In *Time Capsule: Short Stories About Teenagers Throughout the Twentieth Century*. Ed. by Donald R. Gallo. New York: Delacorte Press, 1999. 143–65. In the 1960s, Benny Woods is bullied by his football coach because he refuses to cut his long hair.

———. "Guns for Geeks." In *On the Fringe*. Ed. by Donald R. Gallo. New York: Dial Books, 2001. 195–219. Bullied by teachers as well as classmates for his whole life, Gene Taylor carries a gun to school and starts shooting.

———. "In the Time I Get." In *Athletic Shorts: Six Short Stories*. New York: Greenwillow, 1991. 133–61. Louie Banks has to examine his own homophobia and his friend's when he meets Dakota's nephew, a gay man with AIDS.

Garden, Nancy. "Parents' Night." In *Am I Blue?* Ed. by Marion Dane Bauer. New York: HarperTrophy, 1994. 129–44. Karen joins the Gay-Straight-Bisexual Alliance at school and gets used to the harassment there but isn't sure how to handle her parents' prejudices at home.

Griffin, Peni R. "The Truth in the Case of Eliza Mary Muller, by Herself." In *Stay True: Short Stories for Strong Girls.* Ed. by Marilyn Singer. New York: Scholastic Press, 1998. 109–26. When her sister is beaten by her husband, Bud, and Bud makes advances on Eliza, she defends herself and her sister with her father's rifle.

Lantz, Francess. "Standing on the Roof Naked." In *On the Fringe.* Ed. by Donald R. Gallo. New York: Dial Books, 2001. 89–113. Jeannie feels different from everyone else in her school, and she is, which is why she's picked on frequently.

Lester, Julius. "Spear." In *Places I Never Meant to Be: Original Stories by Censored Writers.* Ed. by Judy Blume. New York: Simon & Schuster, 1999. 37–51. Because Spear, who is black, and Norma, who is white, fall in love, they face nasty comments from friend as and family members on both sides of the color line.

Salisbury, Graham. "Mrs. Noonan." In *On the Fringe.* Ed. by Donald R. Gallo. New York: Dial Books, 2001. 117–41. Not only does Billy Keiffer have to deal with his attraction for Mrs. Noonan, but two senior boys, Nitt and Johnson, take pleasure in making his life miserable.

Weaver, Will. "The Photograph." In *No Easy Answers: Short Stories About Teenagers Making Tough Choices.* Ed. by Donald R. Gallo. New York: Delacorte Press, 1997. 3–24. Anthony knows right from wrong, but it's hard to fight against the demands made by Lance Henderson, the football team quarterback.

———. "WWJD." In *On the Fringe.* Ed. by Donald R. Gallo. New York: Dial Books, 2001. 145–61. Suzanne's religious beliefs are tested when she is faced with continual harassment from Eddie Halvorsen.

Other Books

Some books are also appropriate for middle school (M).

Adoff, Jaime. *Names Will Never Hurt Me.* New York: Dutton Children's Books, 2004. The voices of four teenagers tell the story of one day in the life of their high school, the day when the football hero falls from grace and two of the many targets of the school's bullies act courageously.

Anderson, Laurie Halse. *Catalyst*. New York: Viking, 2002. Kat, a high
    school senior, excels at sports and academics, but pressure to get
    into a good college drives her. She is one of the elite, but she has a
    conscience.

————. *Speak*. New York: Puffin Books, 1999. Melinda describes her
    freshman year in high school following a summer when she was
    raped at a party and so traumatized that she can't talk about it. As-
    sisted by a supportive art teacher, she slowly begins to give voice
    to her feelings. (M)

Atkins, Catherine. *Alt Ed*. New York: B. P. Putnam's Sons/Penguin
    Putnam Books for Young Readers, 2003. Ninth-grader Susan Cal-
    loway is assigned an alturnative to suspension with five other stu-
    dents. One is Kale, the biggest bully in school and another is the
    Brendan, who is believed to be gay.

Bloor, Edward. *Tangerine*. San Diego: Harcourt, 1997. Paul Fisher
    lives in the shadow of his older brother, Erik. Legally blind, Paul
    still manages to play soccer while Erik steals the family's attention
    as a star football kicker. Slowly the truth about Paul's blindness
    comes out in flashbacks of cruelty involving Erik. (M)

Brooks, Kevin. *Lucas*. New York: Scholastic, 2002. Lucas lives a free
    life, an outsider who is comfortable with that position. While most
    of the island youth harass this loner, Caitlin befriends him and
    stands as his only ally.

Brugman, Alyssa. *Walking Naked*. New York: Delacorte Press 2004.
    Megan Tuw is not only part of the eleventh grade in-group, she
    leads it. If someone strays, she calls for an intervention. Megan
    gets assigned detention with Perdita Wiguiggan, the school freak,
    and against every rule of her group, Megan starts to befriend Per-
    dita. (M)

Byalick, Marcia, *Quit It*. New York: Delacorte Press, 2002. Last year,
    Carrie was a happy eighth grader, but over the summer she has de-
    veloped Tourette's syndrome, and ninth grade becomes a night-
    mare. (M)

Carvell, Marlene. *Who Will Tell My Brother?* New York: Hyperion,
    2002. Though Evan has always been conscious of his Mohawk
    heritage, it is not until his senior year in high school that he feels
    the need to take a stand. He does this by asking the school board to
    change the offensive Indian mascot. Though his attempts are quiet
    and follow the established recourse, the harassment he suffers
    ranges from personal verbal attacks to violence against his whole
    family. (M)

Cheripko, Jan. *Rat*. Honesdale, PA: Boyds Mills Press, 2002. When fifteen-year-old Jeremy Chandler testifies against the popular basketball coach for molesting a cheerleader, his relationship with the other students, particularly the team, is destroyed. The new coach challenges Jeremy to still do his best. (M)

Cole, Brock. *The Facts Speak for Themselves*. Asheville, NC: Front Street, 1996. Linda, thirteen, has experienced too much loneliness and responsibility in her young life. She and her two younger brothers, all from different fathers, only survive their mother's reckless relationships because Linda fills the parent role. Using journal entries, Linda explains all that led to the murder she witnessed in the first chapter. (M)

Cormier, Robert. *The Chocolate War*. New York: Pantheon Books, 1974. When Jerry Renault refuses to sell chocolates for his Catholic school's yearly fundraiser, he faces the wrath of the intimidating Vigils as well as Brother Leon.

Crowe, Chris. *Mississippi Trial, 1955*. New York: Phyllis Fogelman Books, 2002. While visiting his beloved grandfather in Mississippi, a white teenage boy meets Emmett Till, a feisty black teen from Chicago, who is soon murdered for whistling at a white woman. (M)

Crutcher, Chris. *Ironman*. New York: Greenwillow, 1995. Bo Brewster has never learned to control his temper, due in large part to the bullying he's received from his father and school officials, so he's sent to an after-school Anger Management class where he meets a motley group of other hard-nosed students.

————. *Whale Talk*. New York: Greenwillow, 2001. Behind the triumphs of a high school swim team composed of misfits lurk painful lives and present dangers that culminate in a shocking and surprising ending.

Dessen, Sarah. *Dreamland*. New York: Viking, 2000. After her older sister runs away from home, Caitlin gets involved in a relationship with a "hot," secretive, and very intelligent drug dealer who later becomes abusive. (M)

Draper, Sharon M. *The Battle of Jericho*. New York: Atheneum, 2003. An invitation to join the Warriors of Distinction, the most exclusive club in school, carries prestige. However, Jericho has uncomfortable doubts when the initation starts—is it all in fun or could this hazing cross the line into danger?

Ferris, Jean. *Eight Seconds*. San Diego: Harcourt, 2000. After his father signs him up for rodeo camp, John finds a competition he's good at—riding bulls. That's easy compared to the friendship he has formed with Kit, his rodeo buddy, who is gay.

Flinn, Alex. *Breaking Point*. New York: HarperCollins, 2002. In a private school, rich students make life miserable for poor newcomers like Paul until Charlie, a school leader, invites Paul into his elite circle. Soon Paul realizes what that acceptance will cost him.

———. *Breathing Underwater*. New York: HarperCollins, 2001. Because he has beaten his girlfriend, Nick is ordered by the court to attend anger management classes and write a journal to explain what happened in his relationship.

Foon, Dennis. *Skud*. Toronto: Groundwood Books, 2003. Told in the voices of four young men, this story shows their struggles to survive manipulation and stereotyping in the difficult environment of high school.

Friel, Maeve. *Charlie's Story*. Atlanta: Peachtree Publishers, 1997. Charlie was abandoned by her mother at age four. Ten years later the cruelty of her classmates who bully her because of that abandonment nearly causes Charlie to end her life. (M)

Friesen, Gayle. *Men of Stone*. Toronto, ON: Kids Can Press, 2000. Fifteen-year-old Ben had a strong interest in dance but gave it up because he was tired of the harassment. Claude's bullying is escalating, and Ben takes up boxing as a way to survive. (M)

Gallo, Donald R. Editor. *On the Fringe*. New York: Dial, 2001. A collection of short stories written by well-known authors who specifically write for teens. Each story focuses on teens who are on the fringe of acceptance. (M)

Giles, Gayle. *Shattering Glass*. Brookfield, CT: Roaring Book Press, 2002. Rob is the charismatic kid who moves to town and becomes the new leader. He manipulates losers into the top clique and former winners into loser status. From the opening page, the reader knows who will die.

Goobie, Beth. *Sticks and Stones*. Victoria, BC: Orca Book Publishers, 2002. Falsely labeled as a "slut," Jujube fights back against the slurs whispered in the hallways and written on the bathroom walls of her school.

Henegham, James. *Hit Squad*. Victoria, BC, Canada: Orca Book Publishers, 2003. Grandview High School has the smartest students. Mickey transfers to Grandview to make a fresh start, but soon he discovers the school is ruled by cruel bullies. He joins three other students to form a hit squad that will set things right. But these ninth-grade vigilantes can't see they are the new bullies. High interet/easy reading.

Klass, David. *Home of the Braves*. New York: Farrar, Straus & Giroux, 2002. Eighteen-year-old Joe is frustrated when a Brazilian student joins their soccer team and starts dating the girl Joe has hoped to date, but it's violence off the playing field that threatens to destroy the school and Joe's future.

————. *You Don't Know Me*. New York: Farrar, Straus & Giroux, 2001. Although fourteen-year-old John says nobody knows the first thing about him, his multilayered thoughts amusingly reveal everything we need to know about his painful life—algebra class, band practice, relationships with girls, and his home life, especially his abusive stepfather. (M)

Koertge, Ron. *The Brimstone Journals*. Cambridge, MA: Candlewick Press, 2001. Using first-person poems from the points of view of fifteen students, Koertge reveals the anger, hate, and longings in a suburban high school that lead to an explosive situation.

————. *Stoner & Spaz*. Cambridge, MA: Candlewick Press, 2002. When Ben, a sixteen year-old cerebral palsy victim and loner, teams up with a drugged, tattooed, rebellious Colleen, his life is changed forever.

Koja, Kathe. *Buddha Boy*. New York: Frances Foster Books/Farrar, Straus & Giroux, 2003. Justin doesn't plan on befriending the weird new kid who calls himself Jensen, but after seeing how others at wealthy Edward Rucher High School treat this newcomer with a shaven head, kind smile, and gentle ways, Justin can't go along with the crowd. (M)

Lekich, John. *The Losers' Club*. Toronto: Annick Press, 2002. Jerry Whitman and the other "haves" make life miserable for the "have-nots" at Marshall McLuhan High School. Alex Sherwood, dubbed Savior by the Losers' Club, has cerebral palsy and walks with crutches. (M)

Lubar, David, *Hidden Talents*. New York: Tor, 1999. At Edgeview Alternative School, Martin and his odd friends discover they have special abilities that get them into trouble but when controlled, can be used for positive purposes—like handling the school bullies. (M)

Mayfield, Sue. *Drowning Anna*. New York: Hyperion, 2002. Anna Goldsmith, thirteen, moves to a new town and a new school. Hayley chooses Anna to be her new best friend, and things are wonderful, until Hayley, suddenly, drops Anna. Told in flashbacks after Anna has tried to kill herself, this book weaves together Anna's journal, her mother's bedside watch, and the reflections of her friend, Melanie. (M)

Mazer, Norma Fox. *Out of Control*. New York: Avon Books, 1993. Rollo Wingate thinks his life was perfect because he has two best friends. The three of them were the Lethal Threesome but following his friends leads Rollo into bullying and harassment. This book gives us an inside view of both the bully and the target. (M)

McNeal, Laura, and Tom McNeal. *Crooked*. New York: Knopf, 1999. Clara has a crooked nose; Charles and Eddie Tripp have crooked lives. Things get complicated in ninth grade when bad, crooked things start hurting good people. (M)

Mikaelsen, Ben. *Touching Spirit Bear*. New York: HarperCollins, 2001. Ordered to participate in a Native American Circle of Justice program as an alternative to jail, Cole is banished for a year to a remote island in Alaska where he is mauled by a huge white bear. (M)

Muharrar, Aisha. *More than a Label*. Minneapolis, MN: Free Spirit Publishing, 2002. Nonfiction. Muharrar was still in high school when she wrote this book, but it isn't an English class assignment. She compiled her research from over one thousand Teens Label Surveys and wove that information with her thoughts—which are pretty down to earth. (M)

Oates, Joyce Carol. *Big Mouth and Ugly Girl*. New York: Harper-Collins, 2002. Matt Donaghy, a.k.a. Big Mouth, and Ursula Riggs, a.k.a. Ugly Girl, develop an unlikely friendship after Matt is wrongly accused of threatening the school with a bomb and Ursula is the only one who stands up for him. (M)

Philbrick, Rodman. *Freak the Mighty*. New York: Scholastic, 1993. Max, bigger than most kids his age, gets called "Stupid" and "Dummy." Freak, tiny and sickly, is brilliant. With Freak on Max's shoulders, they can take on the world. (M)

———. *The Last Book in the Universe*. New York: Blue Sky Press/Scholastic, 2000. In a future time without hope, Spaz tries to rescue his little sister with the help of Ryter and a proov (genetically perfected) girl who lives in Eden. (M)

Plum-Ucci, Carol. *The Body of Christopher Creed*. San Diego: Harcourt, 2000. When one of their schoolmates disappears, most of his peers offer insensitive opinions of why and what happened. Slowly the pain of his life and the way they all bullied him begins to emerge. (M)

———. *What Happened to Lani Garver*. San Diego: Harcourt, 2002. Claire McKenzie tells the story of her friend Lani Garver's brief stay on Hackett Island, where most of the island is trying to decide if Lani is a he or a she. Told in flashbacks, Lani, wise, sensitive, and courageous, died at the hand of the island's rednecks.

Rall, Ted. *My War with Brian*. New York: Nantier, Beall, Minoustchine, 1998. This graphic novel says everything the researchers say about bullying, but it gets the point across quicker. Rall barely escapes middle school with his life thanks to Brian, Rall's own personal bully, but when he reaches high school, Rall refuses to take it any more.

Randle, Kristen D. *Breaking Rank*. New York: Morrow Junior Books, 1999. Casey has agreed to tutor Thomas, a member of the Clan, a rigid, male cult-like group that never mixes with the town kids. Intolerance spreads as their friendship grows. (M)

———. *Slumming*. New York: HarperCollins, 2003. Nikki, Alicia, and Sam are part of the privileged elite circle at their high school. With only half their senior year to go, they decide on a private community service project. Each will take on one of the "less together students" and make that more socially acceptable. As they struggle in these new relationships, Nikki, Alicia and Sam have to look at themselves and their preconceived judgments.

Rapp, Adam. *The Buffalo Tree*. Arden, NC.: Front Street Books, 1997. Thirteen-year-old Sura struggles to survive his six-month sentence in a juvenile detention center with a particularly sadistic inmate. (M)

———. *Little Chicago*. Asheville, NC: Front Street, 2002. This is a very disturbing story of eleven-year-old Blackie, who is sexually abused by his mother's boyfriend and picked on at school, trying to find some peace in his life.

Sanchez, Alex. *Rainbow Boys*. New York: Simon & Schuster, 2001. Nelson is totally "out"; Kyle is keeping the secret; and Jason is trying to come to terms with bisexuality. When Nelson tries to start a Gay/Straight Alliance at school, the homophobia goes public.

———. *Rainbow High*. New York: Simon & Schuster, 2003. In their senior year, the young men from *Rainbow Boys* continue their struggle to be accepted.

Slade, Arthur. *Tribes*. New York: Random House, 2002. After the disappearance of his father, Percy escapes into the safe analytical world of science as he studies the different tribes in his high school: the Jock Tribe, the Born-Again Tribe, the Grunge Tribe, and others. (M)

Slaven, Elaine. Illustrated by Brooke Kerrigan. *Bullying: Deal with it Before Push Comes to Shove*. Toronto, ON: James Lorimer & Company, 2003. Nonfiction. Aimed at students, this highly illustrated booklet is excellent. It discusses all types of bullying and has quizzes and self checks to get the points across clearly. (M)

Spinelli, Jerry. *Stargirl.* New York: Knopf, 2000. A new student named Stargirl celebrates her uniqueness in eccentric ways that stun the students of Mica High School. (M)

Strasser, Todd. *Give a Boy a Gun.* New York: Simon & Schuster, 2000. The events in this timely novel will blow you away with as much emotion as the high school students in the novel experience when one of their classmates starts shooting them at a school dance.

Tashijian, Janet. *Fault Line.* New York: Henry Holt, 2003. While finishing her senior year, Becky Martin haunts comedy clubs where she is in training for her ultimate goal—to be a stand-up comic. Confident, intelligent, and funny, how could she fall into an abusive relationship? Far too easily.

Taylor, William. *Jerome.* Los Angeles: Alyson Publications, 1999. Communicating through e-mails and faxes, Marco in Australia and Katie in the U. S. heal after the hunting death of their friend, Jerome. Secrets are revealed as they piece together what they know.

Tullson, Diane. *Edge.* Toronto, ON: Stoddart Kids, 2002. After joining a group of misfits, ninth-grader Marlie Peters has to decide if belonging to a group is worth giving up what one believes is right. (M)

Weaver, Will. *Farm Team.* New York: HarperCollins, 1995. Billy Baggs loves baseball and has a wicked pitching arm at fourteen, but while his dad is in jail, he has to run the family farm and his mom must get a job. The baseball coach sees Billy pitch and gets him on the team with all the town boys. (M)

Wittlinger, Ellen. *What's in a Name.* New York: Simon & Schuster, 2000. Told by ten different students in Scrug Harbor High School, these stories give the reader a more total view of hidden motivations and hurt feelings than even these characters have. (M)

Woodson, Jacqueline. *Miracle's Boys.* New York: Penguin Putnam, 2000. Three brothers, Ty'ree, Charlie, and Lafayette, try to survive after their mother's death. But since Charlie has come back from Rahway prison, he's changed: he's Newcharlie now. (M)

Yamanaka, Lois-Ann. *Name Me Nobody.* New York: Hyperion, 1999. Emi-lou and Yvonne have grown up together, best friends, self-adopted sisters, closer than family. But suddenly growing up is more like growing apart. Set in Hawaii, the diversity of the islands and the language add to the story. (M)

Chapter Seven

Annotated Bibliography of Selected Resources

While most of my work has been in finding the right book in children/young adult literature for the classroom teacher to use with her students, I have also had to educate myself with the recent literature available on this issue. Title recommendations came from many sources: workshops, individuals, footnotes in the texts I have read, Internet sites, and my Amazon profile. This bibliography is far from a complete list of published works on bullying and harassment of young people. I have read many of these books cover to cover and have used some in my presentation to students and/or professional groups. Some I have only pulled out the information or activity needed for a specific event or to tie in with a particular book I was teaching in my classroom. But my eyes have been inside each of these books, and I have found useful things. Few among you will need all of these, as they cover working with students from kindergarten through twelfth grade. Some refer to studies in this country only, whereas others discuss bullying issues in countries around the world. Your choice will also be influenced by whether you are a parent, teacher, counselor, administrator, researcher, or just a curious person who needs a title for a book group. But whatever your focus, please look beyond this list, as there is still a growing abundance of knowledge out there about bullying and harassment. I'm still looking.

Aronson, Elliot. *Nobody Left to Hate: Teaching Compassion After Columbine*. New York: Worth Publishers, 2000. A close look at the wreckage left after Columbine. There is wonderful knowledge in here. The research gets a bit dry at times, but the gems are worth it.

Beane, Allan L. *The Bully Free Classroom, Over 100 Tips and Strategies for Teacher K–8*. Minneapolis, MN: Free Spirit Publishing, 1999. I have used some of these activities with students of all ages and passed on some of the information sheets to adults. An excellent resource.

Coloroso, Barbara. *The Bully, the Bullied, and the Bystander: From Preschool to High School—How Parents and Teachers Can Break the Cycle of Violence*. New York: HarperCollins, 2003. This book explains the part each of the three—the bully, the target, and the witnesses—play in the bullying event. Everyone carries away pain.

Dellasega, Cheryle and Charisse Nixon. *Girl Wars: Twelve Strategies That Will End Female Bullying*. New York: Simon & Schuster, 2003. This book presents a thorough discussion of Relational Aggression and ways adults can work to prevent it and help those involved.

Donahue, David M. *Lesbian, Gay, Bisexual, and Transgender Rights: A Human Rights Perspective*. Minneapolis, MN: Human Rights Resource Center, 2000. A very needed resource, the activities and information in this publication are intended for high school students and adults. Some can be modified for middle school use.

Elias, Maurice J. and Joseph E. Zins, *Bullying, Peer Harassment, and Victimization in the Schools: The Next Generation of Prevention*. Binghamton, NY: The Haworth Press, 2003. A collection of research papers dealing with the stated topics, most applicable for middle school.

Fahy, Una. *How to Make the World a Better Place for Gays and Lesbians*. New York: Warner Books, Inc., 1995. This was the first book I found to educate myself about homophobia. It is still my favorite.

Frankel, Fred. Illustrated by Barry Wetmore. *Good Friends Are Hard to Find: Help Your Child Find, Make and Keep Friends*. Los Angeles: Perspective Publishing, 1996. A very practical book for parents with young children, it is filled with activities that make sense.

Freedman, Judy S. *Easing the Teasing: Helping Your Child Cope with Name-Calling, Ridicule, and Verbal Bullying*. New York: Contemporary Books, 2002. This book helps parents understand the issue. There are many case studies to back up suggested strategies.

Froschi, Merle, Barbara Sprung, Nancy Mullin-Rindler, et al. *Quit It! A Teacher's Guide on Teasing and Bullying for Use with Students in Grades K–3.* Washington, DC: NEA Professional Library, 1998. Many people do not think bullying goes on in the primary grades. This publication corrects that misconception with information and strategies to help set a tone of respect in the classroom and to deal with the bullying problems that do exist.

Fried, SuEllen and Paula Fried. *Bullies & Victim: Helping Your Child Survive the Schoolyard Battlefield.* New York: M. Evans and Company, 1996. This book gives parents of elementary students information on the problem, things to try, and practical strategies to combat the helplessness most parents feel.

Garbarino, James and Ellen deLara. *And Words Can Hurt Forever: How to Protect Adolescents from Bullying, Harassment and Emotional Violence.* New York: The Free Press, 2002. A parent recommended this book to me and spoke of it with such respect that I ordered it immediately. Each chapter ends with a section titled, "What Can You Do?" Well structured with background, advice, and strategies.

Geffner, Robert A., Marti Loring, and Corinna Young, eds. *Bullying Behavior: Current Issues, Research, and Interventions.* Binghamton, NY: The Halworth Maltreatment & Trauma Press, 2001. This is an excellent, well researched and documented selection of articles focused on middle school that are accessible to those of us who are not research-oriented readers.

Holmes, Ellen White. *Graphic Organizers: Supports Balanced Literacy and Cross-Curricular Applications, Grade 1–5.* Greensboro, NC: Carson-Dellosa Publishing Company, Inc., 2003. I mention using graphic organizers in several of the suggested activities, and there are many books available on this strategy. This book is a good one with color transparencies and black-line reproducibles.

Hoover, John H. and Ronald Oliver. *The Bullying Prevention Handbook: A Guide for Principals, Teachers, and Counselors.* Bloomington, IN: National Educational Service, 1996. One of the best resources I found, this book gives an overview of the problem and reccommends steps to implement an anti-bullying program.

Huegel, Kelly *GLBTQ: The Survival Guide for Queer & Questioning Teens.* Minneapolis, MN: Free Spirit, 2003. This book deals with all issues relating to gay, lesbian, bisexual, transgender, and questioning teens. Check the index for the many pages dealing with harassment.

Karres, Erika V. Shearin. *Mean Chicks, Cliques, and Dirty Tricks: A Real Girl's Guide to Getting Through the Day with Smarts and Style*. Avon, MA: Adams Media, 2004. This book has solid information presented in a style that makes it attractive to teen girls. Through out there are quizzes that will help the reader realize how she might react to mean chicks and cliques.

Kivel, Paul and Allan Creighton with the Oakland Men's Project. *Making the Peace: A Fifteen Session Violence Prevention Curriculum for Young People*. Alameda, CA: Hunter House Inc., 1997. Filled with many effective activities and strategies for working with young people, this is the first place I read the word "Adultism," defined as "the systematic exploitation, mistreatment, and abuse of young people by adults." (73)

Levine, David A. *Building Classroom Communities: Strategies for Developing a Culture of Caring*. Bloomington, IN: National Educational Service, 2003. Imagine teaching empathy and building classroom communities to prevent bullying and other disrespectful behaviors. This book helps to do just that.

Lewis, Barbara A. *Being Your Best: Character Building for Kids 7–10*. Minneapolis, MN: Free Spirit, 2000. A great book with terrific activities for teaching character traits. Parents and teachers will find this book useful. Essays written by kids about each trait brighten the text.

———. *What Do You Stand For? A Kid's Guide to Building Character*. Minneapolis, MN: Free Spirit, 1998. Lewis's first book on building character for secondary students includes activities, resources, Internet sites, student essays, and self-evaluations.

Marano, Hara Estroff. *Why Doesn't Anybody Like Me? A Guide to Raising Socially Confident Kids*. New York: Quill, William Morrow and Company, 1998. A very readable and informative book for parents to help understand the social worlds for children up to middle teens.

McCoy, Elin. *What To Do . . . When Kids Are Mean to Your Child*. Pleasantville, NY: Reader's Digest, 1997. This text provides basic information and tactics parents can practice with their children.

McNamara, Barry E. and Francine J. McNamara. *Keys to Dealing with Bullies*. Hauppauge, NY: Barron's Educational Series, 1997. This was created for parents, but is also valuable for teachers. Good information covering all parts of this issues and activities for dealing with all involved, particularly the bully.

Nuwer, Hank. *High School Hazing: When Rites Become Wrongs*. New York: Franklin Watts, 2000. This book, informative and factual, deals with the history of hazing.

Olweus, Dan. *Bullying at School: What We Know and What We Can Do*. Maiden, MA: Blackwell Publishers Inc., 1993. Olweus is the leading researcher in the world on the problems of bullying; this is one of the first texts discussing this international dilemma.

Perrotti, Jeff and Kim Westheimer. *When the Drama Club Is Not Enough: Lessons from the Safe Schools Program for Gay and Lesbian Students*. Boston: Beacon Press, 2001. An excellent resource for helping students who are gay or are perceived-to-be gay. Gay bashing is the biggest harassment problem in school today. This program provides answers for every question or scenario you can think of.

Roberts, Anita. *Safe Teen: Powerful Alternatives to Violence*. Vancouver, BC: Polestar, 2001. Starting with a belief that both males and females need to learn alternatives to violence, Roberts gives us accessible information, practical exercises, and gifts of insight in her Safe Teen Program.

Simmons, Rachel. *Odd Girl Out: The Hidden Culture of Aggression in Girls*. New York: Harcourt, 2002. Through her research with teen girls, Simmons defines the cliques and social circles that dictate acceptance.

Slaven, Elaine. Illustrated by Brooke Kerrigan. *Bullying: Deal with it Before Push Comes to Shove*. Toronto, ON: James Lorimer & Company, 2003. Aimed at students, this highly illustrated booklet is excellent. It discusses all types of bullying and has quizzes and self checks to get the points across clearly.

Smith, P. K., Y. Morita, J. Junger-Tas, et al. *The Nature of School Bullying: A Cross-National Perspective*. New York: Routledge, 1999. Experts from Europe, the British Isles, North America, and the Pacific Rim report on the problem of bullying in their home countries.

Stein, Nan and Dominic Cappello. *Gender Violence/Gender Justice: An Interdisciplinary Teaching Guide for Teachers of English, Literature, Social Studies, Psychology, Health, Peer Counseling, and Family and Consumer Sciences, Grades 7 through 12*. Wellesley, MA: Wellesley College Center for Research on Women, 1999. Again, great core lessons and informative handouts make this an excellent resource. The age range is large, but many lessons seem more appropriate to the younger students in that range.

Stein, Nan and Lisa Sjostrom. *Bullyproof: A Teacher's Guide on Teasing and Bullying for Use with Fourth and Fifth Grade Students*. Washington, DC: NEA Professional Library Publication and the Wellesley College Center for Research on Women, 1996. The authors present core lessons specifically designed for intermediate students. An excellent resource.

————. *Flirting or Hurting? A Teacher's Guide on Student-to-Student Sexual Harassment in Schools, Grades 6 through 12*. Washington, DC: NEA Professional Library Publications and the Wellesley College Center for Research on Women, 1994. This guide was one of the first resources available for teachers. It has core lessons and research for this age group. An excellent resource.

Stern-LaRose, Caryl and Ellen Hofheimer Bettmann. *Hate Hurts: How Children Learn and Unlearn Prejudice*. New York: Scholastic, 2000. The Anti-Defamation League's guide for adults and children presents research and advice for parents on how to fight the invasion of hate into our children's lives.

Sullivan, Keith. *The Anti-Bullying Handbook*. Greenlane, Auckland, NZ: Oxford University Press, 2000. Another excellent resource specifically directed to teachers and administrators using international resources.

Taylor, Julie. *The Girls' Guide to Friends: Straight Talk on Making Close Pals, Creating Lasting Ties, and Being an All-Around Great Friend*. New York: Three Rivers Press, 2002. I really like this book because of its practical information and hip approach. Hand this to any and all young girls you know.

Wiseman, Rosalind. *Queen Bees & Wannabes: Helping Your Daughter Survive Cliques, Gossip, Boyfriends & Other Realities of Adolescence*. New York: Crown Publishers, 2002. Written for parents, this is also a valuable read for teachers. Well written and well researched, this book is the best resource I have found for learning what is happening in the world of adolescent girls.

Internet Sites

www.bullying.org

Started by Bill Belsey, a Canadian father and teacher, this Web site is a valuable resource. Its purpose is expressed on the home page: "To eliminate bullying in our society by supporting individuals and organizations to take positive actions against bullying through the sharing of resources, and to guide and champion them in creating non-violent solutions to the challenges and problems associated with bullying."

www.bullystoppers.com
Created by Tom Letson, a middle-school counselor out of New Jersey, this site has lots of information and is still growing. It is linked to several other sites and resources.

www.cyberbullying.ca
Also created by Bill Belsey, this Web site will not only help students who are being cyberbullied, but it also gives adults a list of behaviors and warning signs to look for. Every parent should check out this site.

www.glsen.org
GLSEN, Gay, Lesbian, Straight Education Network, is a national organization dealing with many aspects of school life for gay and perceived-to-be gay kids. Not only is there enlightening information about homophobia, but also many resources that will help staff deal with that problem in our schools. This is where we started when we wanted to educate ourselves about forming a high school gay/straight alliance.

www.interventioncentral.org
A comprehensive Web site created by Jim Wright, a school psychologist in Syracuse, New York, this site provides strategies for many needed interventions. Type in "bullying" for the on-site search, and articles, connecting sites, strategies, and more can be accessed.

www.stopbullyingnow.hrsa.gov
The US Department of Health and Human Resources has created this well developed web site to aid schools in developing anti-bullying programs. It is the first government led effort to deal with this growing problem.

Index

About the Author

C. J. Bott, Christie Jo, taught high school English for thirty years and still loved her job when she retired in June of 2002. But it was time to do something more about bullying. It is her hope *The Bully in the Book and in the Classroom,* will help teachers discuss the problems of bullying before they have to discipline the behaviors.

In November 2003, C. J. was nominated by the Ohio Council of Teachers and Language Arts for the NCTE/SLATE Intellectual Freedom Award, and was incredibly proud to receive this honor. She asked, "Could there be a higher award for a teacher than to promote intellectual freedom?"

C. J. lives in Solon, Ohio, with her husband, Don Gallo.